I Am Vie

Edited by: Huy T. Pham

Print Edition, Copyright

Print Edition, License Notes

Acknowledgements

First, and foremost, I'd like to thank my parents. They are the rocks on which I have built the foundation of my very being. Everything I am stems from them. Secondly, I'd like to thank my family and friends, especially Isabella, Quynh, Kath, and Jaclyn, whom have shaped me into the man that I am today.

Thank you to everyone that has contributed to this anthology. What started as a pipedream became a reality because of the multiple people that supported the project. People around the world, whom I have never met, wrote stories, provided monetary support, designed web pages, submitted artwork, and edited entries.

A special thank you to the authors that have entrusted me with their life experiences and sincere words. I hope this anthology does them justice.

Thank you also to the volunteer contributors and editors. Van Dang who designed our amazing website. Quyen Truong who designed our awesome glyph. Kath Tran who graciously checked all the Vietnamese. Kevin Tran who served as our only copy editor (any editing mistakes you see are obviously mine and no fault of his). A special thanks to ChrisTin, the creative mastermind behind the cover and the promo video.

And most importantly, thank you for reading this book. I hope you enjoy it. I hope you share it.

Book Cover Credit

The artistic book cover of a young Vietnamese woman in a traditional ao dai with a mask is a metaphor for the multiple cultural layers she wears. Regardless of where she may live, she will forever be 100% Vietnamese.

The beautiful book cover was photo-painted by ChrisTin Jon Nguyen. We would like to thank our photographers David Tang, Thang Le, and Khanh Bui. We would also like to thank our cover model Vyvian Le and our other models Heidi Huynh, Christina Nguyen, and Diana Ngo.

Table of Contents

Foreword

The Foreword is written by Thien Huynh, the first ever Vietnamese-Canadian nationally syndicated newspaper columnist and TV reporter. His award winning articles have appeared in the Toronto Star, Toronto Sun, Huffington Post, and Thoi Bao Newspaper.

When I was just a kid, my dad bought me a book called *Pride of the Vietnamese* for my birthday. I tossed it away. I wanted a dog instead. Weeks later, there was nothing to watch on TV except the Canadian Football League so I finally picked up the red-covered book and opened it for the first time. I was amazed and inspired by what I read…and it changed my thinking about what it meant to be Vietnamese.

There were pages and pages of stories about Vietnamese all over the world accomplishing things that a young child like me could only dream of. I read about powerful Vietnamese politicians in the United States like Viet D. Dinh, successful actors such as Dustin Nguyen, talented athletes such as football star Dat Nguyen, and famous reporters such as Betty Nguyen. My eyes were opened to the vast potential of our people.

I never got to see another edition of that book, but it inspired me to become a reporter and tell others, outside of our Vietnamese community, about our successes, achievements, and culture. Now over 20 years later, Huy Pham has taken on the mantle to assemble a different collection of stories. These new stories explore what it means to be Vietnamese – and come from writers across various continents, diverse cultures, and backgrounds.

I can't think of anyone more perfect to lead an initiative like this. On paper, Huy is everything a "prototypical" Vietnamese-American young professional wishes to be.

I call him the Triple Threat: MIT engineering degrees, Northwestern Law degree, Kellogg MBA - all before the age of 30. He is every Viet mother-in-law's wet dream.

But what makes him "untypical" is an ambition for wanting to push benchmarks and expectations. Not just for himself, but for all Vietnamese. I will always respect him for walking away from several high paying corporate jobs to chase his dream of becoming a National Basketball Association (NBA) executive. Huy has always dreamed big. And why shouldn't he? The Chinese have point guard Jeremy Lin and executive Richard Cho representing them in the NBA. The South Asians can look to Vivek Ranadivé as owner of the Sacramento Kings. Where is our Jeremy, Richard, or Vivek? That's the question that burns at Huy's heart and inspires him to continually redefine how others, including his own friends and family, assume what being Vietnamese should be.

On the other hand, why are some of us utterly content to get a degree, get a job, get married and never be heard from again? What is it about our culture that causes some of us to be afraid to take risks and dream bigger beyond what it typically means to be Vietnamese in our adoptive countries? Throughout this book, you'll feel the restlessness of an entire generation of Viets from across America, Canada, Australia, and Europe – who all want more and took the chances to accomplish more in their careers and their communities. You'll also see personal stories, humorous essays, and intricate poems offering insight into Vietnamese trying to establish their cultural identity through their everyday lives.

I encourage Vietnamese from around the world to share and support this book for three reasons:

First, all proceeds go to charities such as the Vietnamese Culture and Science Association, Sunflower Mission, and Vietnamese American Scholarship

Foundation - all well established for years of directly helping Vietnamese people in need.

Secondly, this project is a great opportunity to share our culture outside of the Vietnamese community. It is a chance to let our non-Vietnamese friends, media, and decision makers realize the contributions that we have made to our adoptive countries.

Finally, this book acts as an inspirational and educational blueprint for the next generation of Vietnamese raised outside of Vietnam. Projects such as this will not only remind our youth of who they are, but also dare them to dream big and become the pride of the Vietnamese.

Editor's Introduction

Sit back and relax. You are in for a treat. This anthology will make you laugh and cry. These are real, raw stories of the Vietnamese from across the world - stories of our struggles with our culture, parents, expectations, sexuality and life itself. I hope you enjoy reading it half as much as I enjoyed editing it.

The name of this anthology, _I Am Vietnamese_, comes from a scholarship essay that I wrote in 2000, as a senior in high school. Initially, I wasn't going to apply, but after being peer pressured by my friends, I quickly drafted up the essay and sent it off. To my amazement, my story went viral. The essay was picked up by multiple news agencies, and was translated and published in many magazines across the world. To this day, I still receive emails from those inspired by that essay.

More importantly, that essay inspired my personal journey to connect with my Vietnamese identity. The essay contest was organized by the Vietnamese Culture and Science Association (VCSA), where I became a life-long member, also serving on its Executive Board. The essay was sponsored by Duy Loan Le, one of the founders of Sunflower Mission, a non-profit organization dedicated to the improvement of education in Vietnam. I would go on to serve on Sunflower Mission's Board for eight years. In 2003, I co-founded the Vietnamese American Scholarship Foundation (VASF). In 2010, I would receive a lifetime achievement award from VCSA for my contributions to the Vietnamese Community. As a boy initially embarrassed of his heritage, I became a man proud of his Vietnamese roots.

Upon some personal reflection almost 15 years later, I conceived the idea for this collection of short stories. A simple story can change lives. I wanted a collection of stories because my stories aren't unique. The Vietnamese living overseas are a special group of people. We are a people without a land. But, that doesn't mean we don't have a culture. Regardless of our varying grasps of the Vietnamese language and our cultural heritage, we are bounded by our struggles, our values, and our parents' quirkiness.

In our hearts, if nowhere else, we are Vietnamese. This book aims to inspire and connect those like us. To provide a sense of community while we struggle on own personal journeys, and to remind to us that we are not alone. We share the same hardships - overprotective parents, the inability to communicate, the struggle to incorporate western and eastern ideals, and the fear of disappointing others.

As we read personal accounts of those like us, we feel inspired, connected, and like we belong. Once, I felt alone in my struggle for personal identity. I hope that this anthology changes that. We are all Vietnamese. Resiliency runs in our blood.

This is a non-profit project. Since we want the entire Vietnamese community to have access to this collection, the ebook version will be completely free. All proceeds (yes, 100%) from the print version will be donated equally to three worthwhile charities that I have personal, extensive experience with: Sunflower Mission, VCSA, and VASF.

If you have read this book and enjoyed it, please consider donating to the three charities. More information can be found at the back of this book.

Please also consider buying or sending a copy to someone else that may enjoy it!

I Am Vietnamese

By: Huy T. Pham

I sit in solemn silence, wondering if I should even bother with this essay. I am not the ideal Vietnamese child; I am nothing special. English is the language I think in, the only language in which I can express my true emotions. I am an American-born Vietnamese child, proud of my heritage, yet forever attempting to grasp it. I merely know this: my morals and values, instilled in me by Vietnamese tradition, make me who I am today. That is why I write, not to win, but to express my pride in my Vietnamese roots. I am Vietnamese. Sometimes it is hard for me to believe. My grasp of the language is childish at best, and at times I feel inadequate. It is something that I am ashamed of, yet something I hope to rectify in the future. But I know I am Vietnamese. The ability to overcome hardship, to face fear and to succeed is in my blood. As our people have always found light in every bad situation, I was raised to do the same. My ability to speak and write may not be up to par with other Vietnamese children, but my heart and spirit will forever be 100% Vietnamese.

My parents are the best. They have never ceased to amaze me. I grew up in Allen Parkway *[the city subsidized projects of Houston in the 1980s]* alongside hundreds of other Vietnamese families. My parents worked long hours at their jobs to try and provide for my sisters and me. My mother is a seamstress, working 60-hour weeks. My father is a fisherman. He is gone for weeks at a time, doing hard physical labor. Whenever I look into his eyes, I begin to cry. I see a man who could have been so much more. He was among the top students in his class. His teachers told him he was destined for greater things. Yet there he stands, in front of my own eyes, a waste of a man. We never had the father and son relationship I have always craved, but my love for him transcends comprehension.

I wish I could say that I had a great upbringing, but I can't. My parents tried their best, but they were hardly ever around. My sisters and I raised ourselves. Among the three of us, the cooking, cleaning and household chores were divided. We did pretty well but there were some things we missed because of the lack of parents. For instance, how could I learn Vietnamese if my mother came home late every night and my father was never around? Even at a young age, I knew why they weren't around. They loved me, and wanted me to be better off than they were. It was that simple.

So I threw myself into my schoolwork. I tried to be a son worthy of such sacrifices. It has not always been easy. I began school as an ESL student. At a young age, I didn't know how to speak English (or Vietnamese) well. Heck, I was in remedial classes for math as well. Nevertheless, I persevered. In time, I became a better and more capable student. By the time I got into high school, I started to realize my potential. I knew that I could graduate at the top of my class and get into a great college. I also realized that my family was heading into a shaky financial situation. One of my father's fishing boats had been hit by an oil tanker and the total loss was a huge drain. So that's where my dilemma started. I decided not to tell my parents about anything I did academically. Any score I received, any report card I ever got, was hidden from them. If they knew how good of a student I was, they wouldn't have allowed me to work. Yeah, I worked. Ever since I was 16, I worked until seven o'clock on school days, and full time during the summer. I tried my best to balance it with extra-curricular activities, debate, schoolwork and volunteering. All it did was amount to a lack of SLEEP.

But I've been successful. In the past three years, I've found a job I absolutely love. I have been a state and nationally qualified speaker. I have continued my activities in volunteering. Most importantly, I have helped my family and have succeeded as a student. The greatest moment in my life was when I told my parents. For the past four years, they assumed I was just an average student. When I got my acceptance into MIT, I rushed downstairs to tell them. The look on my parents' faces will remain with me always. Their bright smiles made all those long nights worth it. For the first time in my life, they told me that they were proud of me. They looked at me and told me that I was worth their sacrifices. I cried. I finally felt as if I was a son worthy of such great parents.

I realize I am not the ideal Vietnamese child. I may not speak as well as I would like, or write as well as the others. But of my accomplishments, of the hardships I have overcome, of my values and morals that I hold dear, I stand proud. In my heart, if nowhere else, I am Vietnamese.

Chapter 1: Assimilation

(Drawing by Ni Pham)

This chapter covers our struggles to assimilate into other cultures.

Pajama Day

By: Sahra Vang Nguyen

"Tomorrow is Pajama Day!" my preschool teacher Miss Kelly announced. As I sat on the story time rug with the rest of my preschool peers, I looked around to see everyone's reactions. Mikey, a Puerto Rican boy with curly hair blurted out, "Will there be candy?" Miss Kelly responded, "There won't be candy but we will have special treats and games!" I wasn't sure what Pajama Day meant, but at least I knew it was a holiday where we would get treats and play fun games. I didn't ask Miss Kelly about Pajama Day because I didn't want to sound stupid or seem different from the other kids. I already felt different from everyone around me.

I was the only Vietnamese American girl at my preschool. Even more, my parents dressed me like a boy. I had a mushroom bowl haircut, shaved side burns, and tomboy clothes. All the other girls had long hair and wore pretty dresses—they looked like their dolls. I didn't look like anything familiar. Every day I brought my favorite teddy bear to school, named Fatty, to play with in case no one wanted to play with me.

That night, I asked my parents what "Pajama Day" meant; they had no clue. I thought to myself, you're my parents, you're supposed to teach me these things, but you are useless. I decided that I would prepare myself for Pajama Day. I wanted to impress my teacher and the other kids, and show them that I knew how to celebrate Pajama Day, too. So I picked out my best outfit for the occasion: a lime green polo shirt, denim overalls with sunflower print, polka-dotted socks and Little Mermaid velcro shoes.

The next morning I felt proud and pretty, like a million bucks. As I walked into the doors of my preschool, I stepped into a complete shock. All the kids were bouncing around in pink onesies, bunny slippers, Spiderman thermals, and dragging their blankies, feather pillows and stuffed animal friends all over the place. I felt like an alien from outer space who lost her way and stumbled into the Care Bear kingdom. "Didn't you know today was Pajama Day?" Miss Kelly asked, "I gave your mom a flyer." As I suppressed the growing resentment towards my parents, held back my tears, and hid the embarrassment on my cheeks, I responded, "I forgot." From that day on, I never went out of my way to fit in again.

[Sahra Vang Nguyen is a multidisciplinary artist currently based in Brooklyn, New York. She has served as the Director of the Writing Success Program at the University of California, Los Angeles, self-published an e-book titled <u>One Ounce Gold</u>, and been published in the print anthology, <u>Pho For Life</u>. In her free time, she enjoys riding her bike around Manhattan looking for new pizza shops. Her website is: http://www.riotinthesky.com]

Ce Que Tu Manges

By: Kelsey Dang

*In the 19th century, gastronomy writer Jean Anthelme Brillat-Savarin declared, "Dis-moi ce que tu manges, je te dirai ce que tu es." In English, this translates to "Tell me what you eat, and I will tell you what you are."

~~~~~~~~~~~~~~~~~~~

I checked my trays again, admiring the majestic pyramid of multi-tiered jello and the heaps of fluffy, sweet, yellow rice. It was heritage week for the fifth graders, and the culminating event was a tasting day in which each student brought in food representing his or her ethnic background. Unable to stand still, I bounced gleefully next to two of my favorite Vietnamese desserts: *Thạch Rau Câu* jelly and *Xôi vò*, a sweet rice.

There are many types of *xôi*, or sweet rice, in Vietnamese cuisine, but my favorite will always be *xôi vò*, sticky rice made with coconut milk and mashed mung beans. I relied on every ounce of self-control my 10-year-old body contained to avoid consuming all of the rice that sat next to me.

The jelly had been particularly difficult to transport and display because it needs to be consumed when very cold. Consequently, my patient mother had helped me cushion the jello squares within layers of towels and ice to avoid a soupy disaster on this sunny California day. *Thạch rau câu* is made from agar-agar, a gelatinous substance found in seaweed. The tri-colored jelly dessert contains coffee, coconut, and pandan (derived from tropical plant leaves) in individual layers.

In a brief introduction, Mrs. Hamilton, our frazzled instructor, explained that my fellow students would wander freely around the classroom to the various tables, tasting international fare and asking about the country from which the food hailed. I grew excited as my first "customer" approached:

"Hi, Jason!"

"What's that?" he asked, pointing to a quivering cube of thạch rau câu.

"It's jello!" I replied too quickly.

"Is the green part lime flavored?"

"No," I said carefully, realizing that I was rapidly losing his interest. "It's green because it's pandan. It's from a leaf. Do you want to try some?"

"No thanks," replied Jason as his nose wrinkled.

"What about some sweet rice?" I implored.

"What's in it?" Jason wanted to know, eyeing the yellow rice.

"Um, mung beans…?" My voice trailed off as my only customer began to edge away.

"I'm going to go over there," Jason announced as he motioned to a table where a girl was happily passing out mini-burritos.

"See ya later Kelsey."

In the course of the twenty-minute tasting event, eight students wanted to know why my jello was milky white, pale green, or rich brown, but no one dared to ingest it. One brave student tried half a Dixie cup of my mung bean sticky rice before tossing it out. Only Mrs. Hamilton sampled both desserts, and she offered an encouraging, if fleeting, smile as she moved away to prevent two students from experimenting with a Bunsen burner that was ostensibly warming soup. With no true "customers" that day, I watched as fifth graders mobbed the Swedish pancake station and so badly wished I had asked my Caucasian mother to prepare Danish cookies instead of having begged my father to help me procure the special Vietnamese treats that sat untouched behind me on my display table.

I accepted my classmates' wary glances and unsophisticated palettes as rejection: rejection of me and of where my father's family came from. In my melodramatic pre-teen mindset, I told myself that I had always known certain kids could be popular socially, but I never knew the same could be true gastronomically.

What I did know was that Vietnamese jelly meant that sacred time after dinner but before bedtime when my dad would cut away a small slice for me and, after I had slurped down the sliver, he would cut me another, substantially larger portion. My dad was always pleased when I chose thạch rau câu jello for dessert instead of cookie dough ice cream, which—according to his taste—was one of the most revolting American delights. Sometimes I would peel apart each layer of the jelly, enjoying the aromatic pandan, the almost cloyingly-sweet coconut, and the bitter coffee flavors independently. Other times, I would devour the entire rainbow before my mother could protest that the strong coffee element would stunt my growth.

As for the yellow rice, our family only ate *xôi vò* on special occasions, so xôi vò reminded me of noisy family gatherings, of falling off my uncle's couch because I was fighting with my ten cousins for a seat, of incense and foreign words and bowing to elders and *chả lụa*, a Vietnamese pork roll commonly eaten with all types of *xôi*. No matter how much *xôi vò* there was, it was never enough, and there were always fights over which child had received a bigger serving. To this day, I chase every last grain of *xôi vò* on my plate, though I often find myself using a fork instead of chopsticks.

After the heritage tasting event, my brother and I enjoyed extra dessert for over a week since there were so many leftovers. My parents consoled me by telling me that my classmates did not know what they were missing, and finally, years later, I'm inclined to believe them. Many people nod to Brillat-Savarin when they say, "You are what you eat." If that is the case, I'm a bit nutty (like mung beans); sweet in an unusual way (like coconut milk); filled with just the right degree of firmness (like agar agar); and colorful, enjoyed layer by layer or all at once, exactly like thạch rau câu jello.

[Kelsey is attending Stanford University, studying Sustainable Product Design.]

A Musical Epiphany

By Van Dang

Being an 80's baby who was born in the U.S. of A and raised on American history and MTV, it should come as no surprise that I was not fond of Vietnamese music while growing up. The indecipherable wailing coupled with occasional glimpses of ostentatious dance numbers was simply off-putting, and to be honest, embarrassing. The mere thought of purchasing a Vietnamese music album or blaring a Vietnamese song out of the speakers of my car would have been unfathomable, and if it were done, it would have been to invoke a snicker or two.

Beginning in middle school and throughout high school, my musical palette consisted of the subgenre of alternative rock known as grunge, and the deviant offspring of hip-hop, gangsta rap. Maybe it was due to my angst and rebelliousness, but I gravitated to both, especially the latter, intrigued by stories that explored the violent inner-city lifestyles of minority youth, which were fueled by displays of bravado and references to vice. This was in stark contrast to Vietnamese music, which seemed soft and sentimental, dull, and devoid of edge. To me, Vietnamese music was reserved to horrid singing at weddings, karaoke my dad blared at home (which never failed to rattle the walls), and overpriced direct-to-video musical extravaganzas with names like Paris By Night and Asia. I pictured old folks with bad nose jobs yodeling about lost loves and of eras gone by. I couldn't understand it at the time; I couldn't understand it both literally *and* figuratively.

When I entered college, my grasp of the Vietnamese language was passable but it wasn't exceptional, not enough to understand the complexities of metaphors and multiple meanings of words and idioms that the Vietnamese language is known for. More importantly it was my inexperience in life that kept me from being able to fully appreciate what so many of the older generations did. A trip or two back to my parent's birthplace instilled in me a desire to learn about my culture and language. Apart from communicating verbally with Vietnamese-speaking friends, it was the songs, not classes or books that helped me learn. Music that was once incoherent began to resonate with my soul. Lyrics that were deceivingly simple were layered in their meaning. I became spellbound by the poetic prowess of such songwriters as Trịnh Công Sơn, Phạm Duy, and Văn Cao.

Vietnamese music has helped me gain a better understanding of myself and of the loved ones around me, bringing me closer to them. It makes me think back to the smile my grandfather, who in rare moments, would flash as he's puffing away on his cigarettes; of my dad pushing the button on the cassette player to record himself singing his favorite Vietnamese ballad; and of my mom and my grandmother toiling away in the kitchen cooking delectable traditional Vietnamese dishes for us to eat. It reminds me of the intoxicating sights, sounds, and smells of a country where it's not unusual for dreams to be created and shattered, only to be rebuilt. It reminds me of the reflections cast on a puddle by motorbikes speeding by, and of a girl working at the noodle stand, whose eyes are as gentle as her touch. I realize that I've now come full circle because I'm the one being overly sentimental — just like the music that I once dismissed. Who would have thought?

[Van is a graduate of San Jose State University with a BA in Design Studies. Van is a first generation American, born to Vietnamese parents who immigrated to the United States from Laos during the Vietnam War. Inspired by his family, memories growing up, including visits to Vietnam at an early age, Van has developed a love and a passion for learning

about his culture and his history. Van currently lives and works out of the San Francisco, Bay Area. Van is also the creative brain and webmaster of the IamVietnamese.org website. He is also the author of <u>Văn</u> and <u>Burning Incense</u> in this anthology.]

Trotzdem

By: Thi Yenhan Truong

"Trotzdem" is a typical German word; translated into English it means "anyway", "yet", or "however". But reading these translations, I can't help but feel unsatisfied. "Trotzdem" is different from its English counterparts. They're too soft and undefined; it feels like eating pudding when what you really want is crisps. Even "in spite" feels wrong because you can't use it as a stand-alone expression. All of the translations lack the sound produced by the consonant cluster in the beginning and in the middle of the word. I miss the striking sharpness. "Trotzdem" sounds determined, authoritative. I used to think that this was the most powerful word in the world.

~~~~~~~~~~~~~~~~~~

"You ok? You eat right now? How your brother doing?" I was chatting with my dad on Skype. He wrote in his broken German that always made me cringe. My father's skills are far from what is considered "fluent", and my mother's German is not any better. Even after thirty-some years in Germany, they still ask me regularly for help with formal letters to authorities, booking hotels, or reading diagnoses of doctors. They came as boat people from Vietnam with nothing but the clothes on their back. They didn't know much about Germany, let alone about the language.

Once they arrived, they attended a basic language course. However, more schooling fell flat since they started a family early. German is a beast of a language to master even for those who dedicate all their time and effort to it. How much harder is it for those who work long shifts in a noisy factory like my father? How much harder for a mum of four who works as a part-time cleaner while taking care of the kids? Learning German was not a priority; so they stayed on the pidgin level, and thus, I prefer to just chat with them on the phone than on Skype. It sounds like an overused trope, but my parents never arrived linguistically and I sometimes doubt if they ever arrived culturally.

"I have a hard time understanding what your mother is saying," my best friend once confessed when she dropped by after school. It was embarrassing for me. In fact, I felt so embarrassed that afterwards I always made sure to be present as an interpreter between outsiders and my mum and dad. This way, questions had to go past me first so I could reconstruct them into a vernacular they understood. It wasn't Vietnamese per se as my skills have always been limited; instead I used my own heavily German-infused pidgin Vietnamese.

As it is probably typical for many Asian or Vietnamese families, my parents always emphasised how important a good formal education was to be successful in a country that wasn't ours. I managed to get into Gymnasium, which is the more challenging branch of German high school, with ease. They were proud of me. I had access to literature and culture that would stay a mystery to my parents. My favourite books were from modern German novelists like Heinrich Böll, Elfriede Jelinek, and Heinrich Mann. I discussed philosophical and political questions as well as culture with my German peers.

German is not considered a beautiful language, not known for being overly sweet or easy on the ears. Instead it's cerebral and precise. It doesn't tolerate ambiguity, and instead is always to the point with an incisiveness that seems unrivalled. If Vietnamese is my mother tongue, soft, forgiving, and feminine, then German is my linguistic father figure. Usually you don't love it as much as you respect it. And still, I liked German with its complicated meandering syntax and the sheer "epicness" of its marvellous consonant accumulations.

Those consonants were one of the things my parents never managed to pronounce properly. They crippled words, sometimes beyond recognition for those unfamiliar with their way of talking. They left out all those troublesome sounds that wouldn't roll off their tongues easily. Their practical knowledge of the case system stayed rudimentary, limited to the concept of tenses, irregular verbs, and the three genders. However, there was one term they would pronounce as correctly as everyone else.

"Trotzdem."

It must have been all the practice they got by using it so much. They trained their pronunciation just like a muscle: the more they used it, the better they became. And they used it a lot.

"Why can't I have a sleepover at my best friend's? You know her parents and they're even at home!"

"Trotzdem!"

The Vietnamese family structure, with its strong hierarchy and respect for elders, and the word "trotzdem" were an unlikely, yet perfect match. Probably because it was such a useful word when you needed to reinforce your authority beyond argument. It has major implications. "You might have arguments, even good ones, but I have power. As long as I am responsible for you, you do what I say because I know what's right for you." As soon as "trotzdem" was used, the discussion was over. No ifs and buts. I had to abide, end of story. As a child, I gave in because my parents' word was law.

As I grew older, the resistance against all those "trotzdems" grew with me. I questioned things that I wasn't allowed to do, the things I had to do, and rights and obligations that felt different than those of my

German friends. I started to fight back with the rigour that only teenage kids have. Their "trotzdem" felt more and more belittling the longer they insisted on using it instead of discussing matters in the open as if they didn't trust my intellect to process things properly. It was them against me. I hated the hierarchy in a Vietnamese family, the respect that you had to pay the elders regardless if they were right, and the rules that came from a different time and culture.

What I failed to realise back then was the reason why they threw the word at me so generously. It wasn't ill will or a twisted power game. A lot of it was helplessness. I can only assume that they wanted to preserve something that I ignored — the essence of being Vietnamese. They tried to raise me like they were raised: no sleepovers and no teenage flings of course, with strong emphasis on formalised Vietnamese family values. This is what they had learned to be correct and good behaviour, regardless of how my peers and their parents handled things here. Maybe they felt I was veering away from my roots and they wanted me to cherish something that I didn't know was valuable. Maybe they confined themselves to "trotzdem" because they were tired or incapable of discussion.

Whatever the reasons, I don't hold a grudge against them or against the word "trotzdem". I made my peace with their limited German skills and my meagre knowledge of Vietnamese and all the misunderstandings that come with it. They have accepted that I make my own decisions that sometimes lean towards my Vietnamese roots and sometimes more to my German side. But maybe my behaviour is not so much determined by dichotomies of any kind. Maybe it is just my own personality that shows in whatever I do. In hindsight and with some distance from my teenage years, I find it rather ironic that my parents tried to defend Vietnamese values against German reality by using German, particularly "trotzdem".

Baseball

By: Binh Hoang

In my large Vietnamese American family, of which I have twenty aunts and uncles and more than twenty first cousins on just my dad's side, I am the only one who follows Major League Baseball. As a New Englander, I root for the Boston Red Sox.

My parents do not understand the rules of baseball. My mom does not watch sports, except when the Super Bowl is on. My dad watches soccer, tennis, college basketball, and the Olympics, but never baseball. Baseball is the American pastime, but I understand why my parents, aunts, and uncles and so many other Vietnamese Americans shy away from it. It was never a part of their upbringing in Vietnam. For my parents to try to understand baseball is as peculiar as for me to try to understand cricket or rugby.

When I was in seventh grade, two of my younger brothers signed up for the town baseball league. As much as I loved baseball, I could not overcome the fear of getting hit by a pitch, so I did sign up with them. Though my dad and I would watch my brothers' baseball games, my dad did not understand how the games were played. I had tried to teach him the rules before, but he never came around to understanding them. Yet he would still show up to all my brothers' baseball games because that mattered more to him than knowing the rules.

I realized back then that baseball was a cultural divide between my parents and my brothers and me. Baseball brought my brothers and me closer to American culture, but at the same time, it alienated us from our parents and their Vietnamese culture.

***

I remember staying up to watch the Boston Red Sox win the 2004 World Series. I was in sixth grade. My middle school homeroom teacher told us the next morning how special it was that the Red Sox had won. It was the first time they had won in 86 years. The Red Sox had finally broke the curse of the Bambino.

I was not a baseball fan before then. Like my parents, I did not even understand the rules. But the excitement that accompanied the Boston Red Sox World Series run captivated me. I did not know that people could be so passionate about a sports team. I was amazed to see people cry on television after the Red Sox won in 2004. Thereafter, I committed myself to being a lifelong Red Sox fan. I taught myself the rules of baseball by watching hours and hours of baseball games on television. I even bought myself a baseball glove and played catch almost every day in the summer with my brothers.

I clung to baseball and the Boston Red Sox throughout my awkward middle school years. Knowing about baseball made me feel comfortable. I could talk about baseball with the other kids and teachers who were baseball fans like me. I could impress them with my knowledge of the current standings, players' stats, trade rumors, and baseball history. I borrowed books on baseball, watched baseball, and played baseball with my brothers.

Nonetheless, no matter how much I learned about baseball, I was not immune from feeling different in middle school. When a student in my seventh grade science class overheard me talking about baseball with my friend, he came over to me and exclaimed, "Binh! I wouldn't think you knew so much about baseball!" His comment deeply hurt me. I knew that he singled me out because I was ethnically Vietnamese. A Vietnamese American kid who loves baseball—not that common back then and not that common even now.

***

To this day, I still love baseball because it has helped me find my Vietnamese American identity. Unlike my middle school self, I am glad that I am different for being a Vietnamese American baseball lover.

Eventually, although it will not be my parents' generation and not even my generation, for the coming generation of Vietnamese Americans, I believe that baseball will become more widely embraced. One day, it will no longer sound peculiar to hear that a Vietnamese American boy or girl loves baseball. We can be different together. Any Vietnamese American can love baseball.

[Binh is a student at Yale University.]

I Am Bitnamee

By: Tiffanie Hoang

I.

When asked by a stranger, "What are you?" or "Where are you from?" my bà ngoại answers: "Bitnamee, honey (pronounced 'hunneigh')," or "Bitnam, hunneigh."

In the beginning of Bitnamee, my bà ngoại swept her nails up and down my back to help me sleep. She called this làm buồn -- to make tired. In the beginning, my grandma shaped rice to look like the body of a sparrow, which she called "chim chim," to encourage me to eat. My grandmother drank with me in Bitnamee when she made condensed milk with coffee for herself, and condensed milk with hot water for me. She ate with me in Bitnamee when she taught me how to savor the pit of a mango. My whole family kisses in Bitnamee when we put our noses to each others' cheeks and inhale.

II.

In Bitnamee, it is "Cali," not "California." It is "grad-ee-ation," not "graduation." It is Chicken ông già (Chicken Old Man) not Kentucky Fried Chicken. I tap peanuts in a ziplock bag with the back of a spoon to make confetti for our rice. Maggi is magic in Bitnamee. My Bitnamee feet can pick up most small objects from the ground, or pinch someone's calf under a table. In Bitnamee, our English words are imbued with the six tones of the language of our parents, so that asking the question, "so?" becomes something like a three-syllable-long inquiry that, at first, hangs low in the throat and ends with a climb in pitch that is exhaled out the mouth.

III.

The Mid-Autumn Festival, the Moon Festival, Tết Trung Thu, occurs on the 15th day of the 8th month during a full moon on the Bitnamee calendar. On this day, we carry lit lanterns of different colors and shapes. We eat sweets. Children sing a song about the day. One part of the second verse mimics the sounds of a drum and then reads:

Em rước đèn này đến cung trăng / I'm taking this lantern up to the moon

The Bitnamee we made and are making together, I want to take up to the moon -- to Chị Hằng -- our sister on the moon.

Have You Ever?

By: Mai Pham

Have you ever had an experience that made you especially proud of being Vietnamese?

I moved to Houston not so long ago and the shower faucet in my apartment broke. My landlord would not pay for it and after a while, I decided to fix it. My uncle gave me a listing of Vietnamese plumbers in the area. I randomly called a plumber named Le. After a short exchange of conversation and pictures of my faucet problems, we settled on a deal and time. He was flexible; he was ready to come any time that was convenient for me. My first thought was that he must be short on jobs. When he was stuck in traffic on the day of, he called me and updated me on the minutes he would be late. I remember thinking, "What if he is a bad man and I am home all alone?"

Well, he turned out to be a skinny, short Vietnamese man, who wore a simple T-shirt with jeans and worn out sneakers. His drooped eyes could probably use some more sleep. He had a gentle smile. His hands were scrawny, defined by bulgy knuckles.

At first, he thought it would be a simple, easy fix. After five unplanned trips from my bathroom to his van to get more equipment and materials, he probably realized that he got the bad end of the deal. But he persisted and fixed my faucet. As he packed up his stuff, I saw the faucet and asked if he was going to cover the space that was there. He told me the space was non-functional cover that could be bought at any home improvement store for a couple of dollars. I was doubtful and feared that my landlord would not be satisfied and hold me responsible for it, though he guaranteed that it would work.

I gave him the check, but he hesitated and asked me to just pay for his gas. He then asked me to go to Home Depot and buy the covering because he thought that I was unhappy with the work. I declined because I just needed it to function. I asked him to take the check and hurry home to his wife and two kids. After all, 8pm had passed.

Forty-five minutes later, I heard a knock on my door. It was the skinny plumber with a faucet cover. He came in and fixed the space. He could have settled. But he didn't. He said, "I don't feel comfortable if you're not happy. I want to sleep peacefully at night." I was not unhappy with his work, but I was touched deeply by his kindness. I had no cash in my apartment and so I gave him a watermelon. Yes, a watermelon. That's all I had.

When he left, I thought to myself, "Was it because he thinks I'm poor with the way my empty apartment looks? Was it because I am a student? Was it because I put on Vietnamese music for him to listen while he was working? Was it because I'm away from my family and he thinks of me as if I was his son in the Navy?" I may never know what went through his mind for him to be so kind to me.

He never cashed my check. I hope he will one day. Every time I use the faucet, I think of him. I often pray for him and his family. Although he doesn't know it, his act of kindness gave me pride, I am proud to share the same culture as him.

I will remember this story so I can tell my children during bedtime, to remind them that greatness does not just come from our jobs, but rather our greatness comes from how we treat others and express our philosophies through what we do.

The Art of Coin Rubbing

By: Linda Ho Sheen

How would I describe my medicine cabinet? As a healthcare provider, I admit that I have some cringe-worthy items like a silver half dollar and a small tube of *Icy Hot*, the extra strength kind. In the typical American household, these items may seem odd, but in a Vietnamese household, these items are essential for medicinal coin rubbing, or cạo gió.

Cạo gió or coin rubbing can be traced back to ancient Chinese traditional medicine and is still practiced throughout Southeastern Asian. *Cạo gió* simply means, "scratching wind" in English and may be foreign to many American households. Eastern practitioners believe that the scratching will help strip the unhealthy elements from the affected areas that result from aches and pains. Affected areas typically bruise due to the breakage of capillaries in the skin tissue. This bruising effect apparently accelerates healing by increasing blood flow to the affected areas, although the bruises may take 4-5 days to fade.

Growing up in a traditional Vietnamese household, coin rubbing was a remedy for almost all illnesses. My grandmother would use her silver half dollar along with her trusty *Eagle-Brand* green colored oil, also called as *dầu xanh*.

As a child, coin rubbing was nothing but a nuisance. The most irritating part of coin rubbing was the fluctuations between hot and cold sensations and smelling like the elderly from either the *Icy Hot* or *dầu xanh*. In order to circumvent coin rubbing, with every strike of the coin would be an exaggerated cry of pain, followed by intense whining. When the pain was unbearable, instead of using a different treatment for illnesses, my grandma replaced the coin by using the outer rinds of a lemon.

After every coin rub, magically my symptoms would drastically improve.

After becoming familiarized with the process, I earned my rite of passage by coin rubbing others. I was subpar. My lines were never long enough and the gaps in between the lines were too wide. I never applied enough *Icy Hot,* which caused burning and pain. Nonetheless, I was called upon when no one else was available.

I have asked both Vietnamese and non-Vietnamese health care providers in regards to the effectiveness of coin rubbing. All were quick to attribute the efficacy towards the psychological placebo effect and dismissed any other possibilities. Angered by their reasoning, I refused to believe that there was only a psychological component to this ancient health practice. I started to experiment on others to examine if they demonstrated relief of symptoms post coin rubbing. I began my experiment on my easiest and most willing volunteer, my husband.

My husband is Taiwanese and is familiarized with many Eastern health practices. Not surprisingly, even he was skeptical of the effectiveness of coin rubbing. In order to prove a point, each time he felt under the weather, I pulled out my trusty coin and *Icy Hot* . After each session, he would vocalize relief of symptoms. In order to test the psychological component, we would coin rub when we were free of any illness and compared that to when we were actually ill. When symptom-free no red marks were elicited with the coin rubbing. If there were any noticeable markings, the marks were light pink in comparison to the remarkable vibrant red that usually presents with illness. This amateur experiment was replicated several times, yet each yielded the same results. Impressed with the results, my husband has now adopted the use of coin rubbing as a form of supplemental care when he is sick.

Even though coin rubbing isn't widely accepted and understood in Western medicine, there is a reason why this practice still exists concurrently. Regardless of the reason, I will continue to keep my half dollar coin and a tube of extra strength *Icy Hot* in my medicine cabinet.

[As a child with a cold, I remember showing up to grade school after a particularly vigorous coin rubbing session. My teacher wanted to call Protective Services and I had to elicit the help of a kind Vietnamese ESL teacher to explain that these bruises were, in fact, an act of love. I've always wondered how many other Vietnamese children experienced the same thing.]

Chapter 2: Growing Pains

(Author Tri Chiem and his mother outside their first home in America)

This chapter deals with the aches and pains we have growing up Vietnamese.

10535 Hammerly Blvd.

By: Tri Chiem

For most of my childhood, I lived in an apartment complex in West Houston, Texas, in an area called Spring Branch.

The complex sprawled across the better length of a street called Hammerly Boulevard and was demarcated from other places, according to the immigrant school children, by the colour of the roofing (this washed-out "Blue," at the time, which has subsequently transitioned into a tiresome mauve.)

I lived there: 10535 Hammerly Boulevard, apartment 143. My first American home.

It was here that I spent my afternoons, frolicking beneath the green patternings of oak trees—a playful tapestry of shadows and light, collecting acorns, piling dust, running ever-quickly to the wonder of my New America: a world fenced off by metal bars and cajoled by the thrill of streetcars—mostly pick-up trucks and sloppy SUVs.

My family, at the time, lived in a two bed-room apartment that set us back just shy of $500 a month, and even that was difficult. We all slept in the same bedroom, with textured bumps on the wall and full- and king-sized beds placed side-by-side. (The other room was for storage: a bunch of cardboard boxes of things my immigrant parents, risk-averse and nostalgic, refused to throw away.)

It's strange to see this place. I haven't been back there in so many years; but for some reason I know that it will always be part of me.

Sometimes I wonder if my identity is made up of simply places—not even people, but specifically places quilted onto the soul.

I identify sites in my memory so vividly somehow. I can tell you the specific shade of blue the sky was when I had my first heartbreak. And how many clouds. (Robin's egg, 5.) I can regale you with stories of how the crows used to dance on flimsy telephone wires every time I waited for my father to come home from work at half past six every afternoon (carrying his ambulance-red plastic lunch container).

I can recall a lot.

I wish I could tell you how it felt to grow up in this part of the world, but I can't really.

I can only share small stories, maybe provide a few photographs here and there, but that alone is not enough.

The honest truth is I cherish my childhood so dearly. I don't think can let go of it, because letting go of something so rare, so fleeting, so beautiful, would be like letting go of the part of me I won't ever get back. It leaves this strange emptiness inside of me; it bleeds at the edges, and it hurts so bad because I know it's made me into the man I am today.

When I remember my time growing up in a working-class Vietnamese family, living in this place, I have the fondest memories. I am proud of them, like they represent a badge, or a heirloom, or something I cannot do without.

I had so many friends who would play with me. For the most part, everyone who lived in the complex were either Vietnamese or Nigerian, but our paths were similar, our stories of diaspora and wanting, inextricably clasped, like twine.

My friends, maybe a year or two my junior, would play Vietnamese jump rope with me (even though they weren't Vietnamese at all, but Nigerian).

We would play jump rope until twilight bruised the sky all sorts of violet and crimson, and I would rush home in hurried breath to watch *I Love Lucy*.

Childhood is always a time of innocence, and it seems cruel that we've departed from it.

Whenever I think of those days, I still feel the triumphant sun beating down the back of my neck, pulsating glowing rays, pouring droplets of sweat onto the fabric of an oversized tee shirt. Heat.

It's easy to fall into the trap of slipping into nostalgia: to think, "how simple those days were then." But those days had their own worries, their own misfortunes, their own sadnesses.

It's difficult to express fully what I mean, but I guess it's something I've kept hidden for so long. I feel as if no matter how hard I try to erase that part of me, that part that sets me apart from my peers at Harvard or Stanford, it will always be part of me. A part of the page written in cursive I can't fully erase because I pressed the pencil too hard.

I live a different history, experience a different world because of these experiences. I guess that's why I don't take anything for granted in this world. It's easy to fall victim of the comforts of our modern time; but I am so aware of the long journey of life, and I know that there's so much more to come.

No matter how far I go, I'll always return to 10535 Hammerly.

Photographs reiterate something I've always known: I

love my family, my roots, my memory. Even as a young boy, I knew the value of photographs, how they have this charge, this power, this ability to ossify the living into the past; the way they can etch something transient into the tablets of life and history. I loved taking photographs, even if my front teeth were rotten and broken, because I knew they would someday end up in a repository of my own memory. It's so strange and exciting to review these old photographs, as if I can somehow engage in a dialogue with the younger, more pristine, version of myself.

If I were there, by the car, talking to that young boy in the cyan cat sandals and holding that conspicuous plastic Batman bag, I'd probably ask him what his dreams were. Did he have dreams at all? Did he want to be an artist? Did he ever think about leaving this place? To see the world? Leave it all behind … the gasoline-soaked pavement… the smallness of life… here?

Most of all, I'd ask him if he'd be happy if he grew up to be the man I am today. I kind of don't want to know the answer.

At a young age, I enjoyed interior spaces only for the promise of the television set: a small 18" JVC tube slightly bigger than my torso. I'd sprawl out on the linoleum kitchen floor or the threadbare denim-colored carpet and watch video cassettes of Vietnamese music variety shows (like Paris by Night). And if I was feeling particularly scholarly, I'd throw in "Speak to Me," a English language tutorial set that went over basic vocabulary words: a video package system that my mother purchased in Night School to learn the new language.

I knew that to make it in America, I'd have to master the English language. And I worked painstakingly hard at it.

I wish I still had those 70-page lined spiral notebooks with all those half-finished stories. I guess not much has changed: I still can't finish a story.

Isn't it weird how time seemed to move slower when you were little? I always thought that a minute, an hour, a day were longer back when I was young, but I realize now that time is so relative to the textured life and experiences you've already had. I guess at twenty-six, a year doesn't feel that significant any more, but when you're five, it was almost your entire life.

I hope I never lose this curiosity about the world. I used to look at the world so interestedly, but lately I've felt removed. As if nothing in this world interests me anymore. As if I had no great question to beg to the universe, and no desire to probe for an answer. This isn't good.

I miss the person I was. I miss that place.

All of this is kind of silly, and I don't know the point of telling you where I've lived. I mean after all, these are just recollections of the early 1990s. But I guess they signify a moment, a special moment. A moment of truth. Of honesty. Of authenticity. Of the world untethered to the trappings of work, greed, and ambition.

I want you to know the person I was, not the person you think I am. I want you to know where I come from. I would hate for you to think I'm something or someone that I'm not.

[Tri Chiem is a graduate of Harvard University. He wrote his senior thesis on the origins of Pho. He would go on to obtain his JD from Stanford University and is currently a lawyer in New York City.]

Art, Weights, and Heartaches

By: Hung T. Pham

As the eldest son born of two Vietnam War refugees who raised a family on love, pride, and food stamps, I was a lot larger than most kids my age growing up, and not in a good way. McDonalds, Taco Bell, and Chinese take-out made dinner for my family affordable because fast food came cheap and in large quantities. In grade school, kids teased me for my weight, calling me names like "dumpling boy," "hippo," and "fatass." "Fatass" hurt the most. And I thought I deserved it, too. I thought that it was my fault because my family didn't have the means to always eat healthier foods that often came too pricey for us. At twelve years old, I was convinced that I was ugly.

In middle school, I started running three miles every single day and secretly forced myself to vomit after dinner, because I wanted to lose weight and become someone worthy of friends rather than of petty fat jokes. And I got skinny, all right. After first semester of eighth grade, I got so thin that kids at my school, the same ones who had teased me for being big, started calling me "toothpick" and "anorexic Asian" and spread rumors that my parents were upset with me and left me to starve at home. To save myself the trouble of high school, at fourteen years old, I contemplated taking my own life the summer before ninth grade started.

Thankfully I didn't, and now here I am at Yale. I'm a healthy young adult majoring in History of Art. I'm not an artist in the classical sense: I don't paint; I can't sculpt; I draw stick figures that are just sad. But when I started bodybuilding in the beginning of last year—because I was so angry with myself for constantly seeking approval from others rather than giving validation to myself—I became my own type of artist.

In a way, the weight room is my studio, the barbell is my paintbrush, and my body is my canvas. The weight room enables me to be unapologetically me and, quite literally, chisel out my destiny. Unfortunately, I think the general public often misunderstands the benefits of bodybuilding and mixes them with the relatively recent stereotypes of an aesthetically pre-occupied, morally shallow culture. But bodybuilding isn't about excessive narcissism, or constructing false perceptions of physical perfection, or constant self-criticism. It's about having a dream, it's about formulating an individualized goal, it's about executing a plan without compromise and, above all, it's about knowing the very real value of pure hard work and sweat.

The next time you exercise, dig deep within yourself and ask questions not of what you are but of who you are. You, and only you, matter in that moment. Invest love and emotion into improving your body for you and not modifying it to fit social expectations.

Bodybuilding reminds me that what truly matters at the end of the day is not what others think of you or whether or not you have external social approval, but rather your unique spirit, the love of those around you, your gratitude, the things that you are good at, the quiet parts inside that deserve to be shared out loud with the world.

Be reminded that each and every one of us is also a work of art created with the many brush strokes of failures and successes, of families, of laughter, of culture, of stories yet to be told, and of indefinable beauty. And to anyone who tries to make you feel less beautiful than you know yourself to be, to anyone who tries to add a paint stroke that would disrupt the colorful harmony already thriving within your frame, roar at them, "This masterpiece is for viewing only. Do not touch."

[Hung is originally from California and is a pre-med student at Yale University. He is also the author of Brick and See, Smell, Taste, Hear, Feel in this anthology. Hung is not blood related to me, in fact we just met through this project, but we are brothers just the same.]

What does 'Vietnamese' Really Mean?

By: Dan Nguyen

I am a soon-to-be college graduate with my whole life ahead of me. How will I make a living, where will I live, who will I marry?…And what will I eat for lunch tomorrow? I have none of those questions about my future answered at the moment. But one thing I know for sure is I will be an advocate of our Vietnamese American community no matter where I end up. I am fiercely proud of being Vietnamese. From something as simple as our mouth-watering spring rolls to the courage amidst adversity that defines our people, there are so many things about Vietnamese culture that I have grown to love.

First is always family. I am very fortunate to have a childhood surrounded by a loving sister, parents, and grandparents. When mom and dad were working, I was raised by my grandparents who didn't speak a lick of English. We would spend the whole day watching kung fu dramas; therefore, I was able to learn how to speak Vietnamese and kick ass very well. And as I grew older, other things we did together as a family continued to teach me about our culture. *Paris By Night.* Chè. Tết. I can recall so many wonderful memories spent with my loved ones. At the root, I think I cherish our culture this much because it embodies the experiences I've shared with my family.

When I hit middle school, my parents decided to enroll me into Vietnamese classes at Trường Việt Ngữ Hùng Vương. As everyone knows, during those awkward teenage years, we all thought we were too cool for school so I was not looking forward to this. But it turned out to be the most fun I had every week. We joked around in class, snuck into PTO meetings for snacks, played games, and had a great time. I also learned how to read, write, and speak Vietnamese. I learned about our holidays, traditions, and history. I was able to gain so much from my time at Hùng Vương because of how the teachers allowed us to participate in class. My cousin Quang and I were certified class clowns all the way through graduation, but we are also the top two performers in our class every year. I even won a Vietnamese essay contest by writing a love letter to my idol, Minh Tuyết. Looking back, I treasure the time I spent at Hùng Vương so I really encourage everyone to go to Vietnamese school.

I attended Camp Lên Đường in 2010, put together by the Vietnamese Culture and Science Association. This was my very first experience at a conference-type event where participants attended workshops, took part in group activities, and met each other. I learned so much about personal development, but the lasting impression that has stayed with me until this day is the scope of our Vietnamese community. There were people from all walks of life. High Schoolers, college students, working professionals, and most notably my Team Counselor, Huy Pham. We were all tied together by our common thread of Vietnamese heritage. I gained a new perspective on the schism that exists between American and Vietnamese born members of my generation. At camp, we all became good friends and came to understand each other despite our different upbringings. This gave me hope and motivation to develop a similar community in my future.

During the summer after sophomore year, I went on a medical mission trip with Project Viet Nam Foundation. I travelled with sixty fellow pre-health students and thirty professionals to hold clinics in various sites of southern Viet Nam. Together, we helped over 2,500 people who had limited access to healthcare. This trip had a profound effect on me because I was able to see our homeland through my own eyes for the first time. I saw our people. I experienced what authentic really means. And I will never forget the images of the patients; the curious eyes of children, the pain, and the smiles of appreciation. One instance that defined my trip was the greatest act of love that I have ever witnessed. There was a gentleman who had a neural disease that paralyzed his lower body. His wife, hoping that American doctors could help, carried him for three whole miles up a rocky, sloped road. The trip took her almost two hours, but she did it. And I was awestruck. Although we of Vietnamese descent do not openly say how we feel about each other, we find other ways of expressing our feelings that speak louder than any words can.

Now onto the most relevant thing to me: the Vietnamese Student Association (VSA) at UT Dallas, where I have had the honor of serving as VSA President for two years. The best way to describe what VSA means to me is well...it's like a girlfriend. I spend a lot of money on her, she stresses me to no end, but she makes me very happy. VSA is a HUGE part of my life because we have built a family amongst our members. We have a community that fosters friendship, volunteerism, school spirit, and laughter. Most importantly, as a part of VSA, I am able to share my love for our Vietnamese culture with friends and the University at large, through our interactive meetings, social events, and campus-wide events that celebrate the Mid-Autumn Festival and Lunar New Year. VSA has been an outlet for me to show my pride as a Vietnamese American.

From my experiences, I learned that culture begins with my family. I learned what makes up our culture at school. I learned who it reaches during my mission trip and camp. And I learned how culture is applied through VSA. So what does *Vietnamese* mean to me? It means family, simplicity, education, food, community, fun, bravery, love, and pride. As Vietnamese Americans, we have a unique situation that we can take advantage of. If we develop our own meaning of being Vietnamese and apply it to how we live in America, our lives will be that much more fulfilling and worthwhile.

I hate being Vietnamese

By: Fong Tran

I hate being Vietnamese
Cause growing up
every Vietnamese dude in my neighbourhood
Was trying to be that same cigarette smelling,
hair slicked back, White T, Baggy Jean wearing
gangster wanna-be
that had that Asian stereotypical tattoo of that
Dragon clashing with the phoenix, or some sort of big
ass Koi fish
or a Chinese Character on his shoulder that stood for
Strength or honor
Homie – that's not even our language

I hate being Vietnamese
Cause growing up
Every Vietnamese dude
Had the same car
Honda Civic, Honda Accord,
Honda Prelude, Honda Hatchback, Honda something
Maybe an Acura Integra
But that's still made by Honda but whatever I digress
The most important part
That yo rice rocket had to be lowered
on to some 15 inch silver spider plastic rims
And I hated how they had to go up on speed bumps at
an angle
so they didn't have to scraped the chassis
I hated how everyone could talk about cars but me
you got to get the S300 Intake manifold turbo
"yeah you know, you know….no…I don't know what that
is"

I hated being Vietnamese
Cause growing up
Every Vietnamese dude
Had the same hair cut

And they were all inspired by Dragonball Z
Either you the Goku Super Saiyan Spikey hair
Or the slicked all the way back
glistening from quarter of a pound of gel
with the Golden Gohan bangs in front
Or the Trunks split down the middle drew
Or the Bulma bowl cut hair
Or you just look like Kirlin
and you were just bald
but to be a true Vietnamese gangster
you had dragon ballz haircut

I hate being Vietnamese
All Vietnamese dudes smell like fish sauce and Pho
You can't be going to the club
smelling up like fish sauce
It's not a good look, bro

I hate being Vietnamese
Cause the Vietnamese men that I knew
Either smoked too much
Gambled too much
drank too much
got shot up too much
abandoned me to be on own too much
like my cousins
like my uncles
like my brothers
like their friends
like my own father

I hated being Vietnamese
Cause all the Vietnamese men in my life
Beat on the Vietnamese womyn that I loved in my life
like my big sister
like my brother's girlfriends
like my own mother

I hated being Vietnamese
Cause being Vietnamese
meant I hated everybody else

hated Hmong people
hated Lao people
Mienh people
Khmer people
hated Black people
Hated everybody
we gangbanged on ourselves
So maybe I'm just as Vietnamese
as I hate to be

But yet I still…
I hate being Vietnamese
because I everything that I was told to be successful
by my teachers, television, society
was everything Vietnamese was not
so being a little boy
"Denying being Vietnamese" was everything I was
taught

I didn't speak Vietnamese
I didn't have Vietnamese friends
I hated being Vietnamese

I wrote off my identity like Standardized Test exams
Not really understanding everything about
my History & my Language
was everything I am

so I took a retest and saw
hating being Vietnamese
was just hating myself
It was self-hate
It's been a language whispered colonist oppressors
Told us to blanket our pride
Never show our true strength
And this generation will simply be the successors
The successors of imperialized slaves
cause in this time, the game has changed
They tell us to be color-blind
No history, no ethnicity, just American

But we chose, we chose to redefine
I don't know about you
But I am Southeast Asian
I am Southeast Asian Vietnamese American
And I know I said I hated being Vietnamese
But at the time
I didn't know what it meant
to be in a family of Warriors and refugees
I didn't understand why Americans helicopter dropped
us
In section 8 housing of violence and poverty
I didn't why broken education systems were at war
and my brothers were the causalities
they drop out of school, learn the gang rob
cause no ever taught them English or how to get a job

I have one message for fellow
Southeast Asians
Be proud of who you are and
Remember where you came from

Remember, we share this narrative of struggle
We are the descendants of generals, kings, dragons
and goddesses
And they say we carry the history of our ancestors on
our backs
So maybe that's why we bear dragon tattoos on our
shoulders
So we can always remember who we are and stay on
track

Maybe that why we leave hints of old aged fermented
fish
or spicy salad sting of jungle decorated papaya
And the beautiful concoctions of curry and coconut milk
in Ka Poon
we leave legendary legacies
Off the simple utterance of our breath

Maybe that's why we bought Hondas
because they were the very engines
that kept fish boats moving
across Southeast Asian seas
to Refugee camps
Maybe that's why we pretend to be thugs
cause our parents were original gangsters – OG's
while we strap guns
they strap farm machetes and hmong knives
through turfs called sun beating rice plantations
they real rick ross bosses
always knew how make my banh mi's
with that pate spread and the soy sauces

Southeast Asian moms had the power to heal all
That healing power was called
Tiger Balm
Vietnamese people called it "Dầu Xanh"
The stuff cure everything
stomach ache, headache, heartache, diarrhea, toe
fungus, gingivitis

Our parents are Super Saiyans
They were the supreme Kai
landscaping, farming. Donut shops, nail salons
They did anything for us to survive
They ascended past super saiyan 4 and 5
Through Frieza's global annihilation attacks
that we call the Cambodian Genocides
Thru Vegeta's hostile takeover disguised as
American assimilation
They will be kamakema fires
The Ginyu Force at our graduations

Graduates, as you make way onto your Goku journeys
to the real world
In search of your 7 dragon ballz
Remember, we will accomplish all that our families have
set out for us to do
And as long as you remember to never ever hate who

you are and embrace your legacy
We will finally be able to grant them
their one wish

[Fong's spoken word craft is even stronger as a performance. His YouTube performance is found at: https://www.youtube.com/watch?v=FJAecUKJ--8. Fong currently serves as the Program Advisor/Coordinator for the UC Davis Cross Cultural Center and is a Masters student in the UC Davis Community Development Graduate Group. His poetry gives voice to marginalized peoples and shares stories of the beautiful struggle that we call life.]

An Endless Ocean of Possibilities

By: Betty Dang

The boat slowly rocked into the dark night. Pirates captured our boat yesterday. Our group quickly smeared dirt on their faces. We were lucky. They let us live to drift into see the sunrise. Now, we drift into a dark, endless ocean. It was dark down below the boat, as I sat between my mom and dad. I remember drifting in and out of sleep.

"We spent 6 months in Thailand before my parents and I came to Hartford," I told our neighbor, finishing up the last detail I remember of my journey to America.

My Caucasian neighbor smiled and turned to my mom, "She's quite an active two year old with such a great memory."

My mom laughed and replied, "She listens to us tell our stories and the crazy girl has it stuck in her head that she traveled here with us. Eight days on the endless ocean. She was born in Hartford Hospital just five minutes away."

My peers and I are a new generation bridging the gap between our Vietnamese culture and our sense of belonging in America. These courageous stories of how my parents had survived a trip into the unknown and found their way to land of the free shaped my childhood. I forgot them for a better part of my 20's. Now, as I step into my 30's, I find a renewed inspiration in these stories, a reminder that I come from a community of strength and courage. We must not forget the generation before us that risked their lives in the endless ocean to find freedom in this new land. Our life moments shape us and lead us down an exciting path. As I go through life I find the pieces of Vietnamese and American to define me.

At age 5, my family and I lived in a run-down building in Hartford. I remember jumping on chairs as rats ran through the living room. I loved going to the corner library to see all the picture books. Even in poverty, my mom made sure I had access to books. Later, we moved into the projects, where the elementary school had more white kids to black kids. Therefore, the school was better than Hartford. That's exactly how my parents explained it to me.

At age 17, I lugged my suitcases up to my corner dorm room that opened into Washington Square Park in New York City. I had listened to my parents and found the best school with the most white kids. New York University. It was an exciting day for a small town girl to be in the big Apple with all these other students. Apparently, Joshua Jackson, Pacey from Dawson's Creek, was at the dorm across the park, helping his sister move in, too!

A week after moving into NYU, I witnessed the aftermath of 9/11 and the collapse of the World Trade Towers. Fear rushed through me, as massive dark clouds of smoke filled the blue skies. The campus had turned into an Independence Day movie scene, groups of students huddled together listening to the radio news. When night finally came, my new friends and I gathered with strangers in Washington Square Park for a candlelight vigil. I cried tears for the lives lost and the wars that would come after this day.

At age 26, I signaled for another card. The dealer smiled as he opened a 5, making my 16 extra special: 21 wins! I always hit on 16 unless I am trying to change my shoe. Don't be a chicken! The dealer matched my stack of black chips and I tossed him $50. It was one of my favorite dealers and he was getting me rich fast. Blackjack was my favorite game. Mohegan Sun was my favorite casino. Everyone remembered me in this pit. A young Asian girl sitting at the $100 tables, big tipper, rolling with the big boys. Bottle service, high-end hotels, spontaneous trips, and shopping sprees. This was what the good life was about.

Rewind. How did I end up at the gambling tables? When I had reached the age of 12, my parents discovered the taste of luxury at Foxwoods Casino and Resort. By the time I had reached the age of 15, I was sick of weekends and holidays at the casino. My parents disappeared for the weekends, mesmerized by the thrill of the tables. The Vietnamese has a passion in their blood for gambling. There's even an Asian Player's Club and an Asian VIP lounge! All the Vietnamese parents I knew took their kids to the casino for "vacation" every other week.

I left home for college as an escape from feelings of abandonment, hurt, and broken promises. I would never make the same mistakes my parents made. I had a brighter future. I was an American, not an immigrant. At the end of college, I had experienced a series of obstacles that led me into a depression. I came back to my family for comfort and found myself making more Vietnamese friends that had just started to enjoy the adrenaline rush of gambling. Before I knew it, I had spent 7 years in a serious relationship with my Player's Card. Sometimes it abused me and left me with nothing, sometimes it gave me a new Coach purse or a box of Godiva chocolates.

At age 29, I look back at my life and career. New York University. PricewaterhouseCoopers. Mohegan Sun Casino. Single. Connecticut. Single. Snowboarding. Single. My life had come down to a collection of words when I moved to Denver a year ago. When I discovered snowboarding a few years ago, it had uplifted my spirits and given me a new chase of adrenaline. However, it didn't change my group of friends and the every so often call of the tables. My social security statement calculated that I had earned my first million dollars, but my credit cards stated I was paying them life. My life had spiraled downwards to hit rock bottom, shattering my heart into pieces. I needed a new start, so I followed my new passion, snowboarding.

The great mountains reminded me how big and unlimited the world is. I found love and a relationship that grounded me. My insecurities and misunderstandings of my childhood had led me into the comfort of gambling. As I raised my self-awareness and experienced an increase of confidence, I gained control of my life and desires. I realized gambling was my escape, but I had more potential than hitting two blackjacks in a row. Healing my heart made me see how I had limited my views due to those around me being stuck. My family had grown apart from broken promises, blame and guilt. My heart has forgiven those moments that took our past. I see that I can help my family move forward into the same space to leave behind their addiction of gambling.

At age 30, I have returned to my home community, to my Vietnamese people. My friends are excited to have me back. They are in full support of my goal to develop a program that helps our people break the cycle of addiction to gambling. It is designed with our cultural differences in mind. I will remind our people of the sacrifices made and strength they had in their journey to find freedom. Together, we will start a new journey to re-shape our lives and explore this new ocean of endless possibilities.

My American Beginning

By: Andrew Lam

For years, on my writing desk sat a framed little card, yellow with age, and it told of my American beginning. It's a picture of a sloop, and under it the word "Sailboat" is written, Mr. Kaeselau, my first teacher in America, gave it to me along with a deck of similar cards many decades ago when I was in seventh grade, and fresh from Vietnam.

The only English I knew back home was "no money, no honey," and "Ok, Salem." I learned it from the loud Saigon prostitutes who walked the tamarind tree-lined boulevards near the Independence Palace - across from which stood my school where I was taught Vietnamese and French.

Back then I thought English was a rather terse and ugly-sounding language -- you don't have to say much to get your points across, but speak it too long you risk hurting your throat. In America that fear became true. A few months after having arrived to San Francisco, my voice started to break. The youngest in my family, I went from a sweet sounding child speaking Vietnamese to a craggy sounding teenager speaking broken English. "You sound like a hungry duck," my older brother would say every time I opened my mouth and everyone laughed.

But not Mr. Kaesleau, who took me bowling with some other students and sometimes drove me home. He had a kind face and a thick mustache that was quite expressive, especially when he smiled and wiggled his eyebrows up and down like Groucho Marx. He gave me A's (which didn't count) before I could put a complete sentence together, "to encourage me," as he would say. At lunchtime, I was one of a handful of privileged kids who were allowed to eat in his classroom and play games -- speed, monopoly -- and read comic books or do homework. It was a delightful sanctuary for the small kids and the "nerds," who would sometimes get jumped by the schoolyard bullies.

For a while I was his echo. "Sailboat," he would say while holding the card up in front of me, and "sailboat" I would repeat after him, copying his inflection and facial gestures. "Hospital," he would say. And "hospital," I would yell back, a little parrot.

Within a few months, I began to speak English freely, though haltingly, and outgrew the cards. I began to banter and joke with my new friends. I acquired a new personality, a sunny, sharp-tongued kid, and often Mr. Kaesleau would shake his head in wonder at the transformation.

How could he have known that I was desperately in love with my new tongue?

I embraced it the way an asphyxiated person in a dark cellar who finally managed to unlock an escape hatch. At home, in the crowded refugee apartment my family shared with my aunt's family, we were a miserable bunch. We wore donated clothes, bought groceries with food stamps and our ratty sofa with its matching loveseat came from a nearby thrift shop.

I remember the smell of fish sauce wafting in the air and adults' voice reminiscing of what's gone and lost. Vietnamese was spoken there, often only in whispers and occasionally in exploded exchanges when the crowded conditions became too much to bear. Vietnam ruled that apartment. It ruled in the form of two grandmothers praying in their separate corners. It ruled in the form of muffled cries of my mother late at night. It ruled in the drunken shouts of an aunt whose husband up and left her and their four children.

In that house, overwhelmed by sadness and confusion, I fell silent. When my father, who had escaped Vietnam a few days after us and managed to final joined us in San Francisco a few months later, things improved. Within two years we even took our first vacation to Lake Tahoe and Disneyland and in another, we will have moved to our first house in America, our humble American dream.

But by then I had practically stopped speaking Vietnamese all together, becoming as mother said, "A little American." It could not be helped. There was something in English that was in stark contrast with Vietnamese. The American "I" stands alone where the Vietnamese "I" is always a familial limitation, the speaker is bound by his ranking and relations to the listener. In Vietnamese there is very little use for impersonal pronouns. One is son, daughter, father, uncle and so on and it is understood only in the context of the communal and familial whereas the American "I" -- as in I think, I feel, I know, I disagree -- encourages personal expression.

It would take me a long, long time before I would embrace my Vietnamese again, balancing the American "I" with the Vietnamese "we," but that, as they say, is another story.

In our refugee home, speaking English was a no-no even if speaking English had already for me becoming second nature. And sometimes, at dinnertime, I would spontaneously sing out a tv jingle with my craggy voice: "My baloney has a first name. It's OSCAR. My baloney has a second name..." The entire family would look at me as if I were a being possessed. Needless to say, my parents constantly scolded me.

Then one day my brother said with a serious voice. "Mom and dad told you not to speak English all the time, and you didn't listen, now look what happen. You shattered your vocal cord. That is why you sound like a duck."

Since no one bothered to tell me about the birds and the bees, I fully believed him. I was duped for what seemed like a long time. But I remember being of two minds: while I mourned the loss of my homeland, I, at the same time, marveled at how speaking a new language could actually change me. After all, I was at an age where magic and reality still shared a porous border, and speaking English was to me like chanting magical incantations. It was indeed reshaping me from inside out. I was enchanted by the English language, its power of transformation, and that enchantment, I am happy to report, had never gone away.

When I graduated from junior high, I came to say goodbye to Mr. Kaeselau and he gave me the cards to take home as mementos, knowing full well that I didn't need them anymore. That day, a short day, I remember taking a shortcut over a hill and on the way down, I tripped and fell. The cards flew out of my hand to scatter like a flock of playful butterflies on the verdant slope. Though I skinned my knee, I laughed. Then, as I scampered to retrieve the cards, I found myself yelling out ecstatically the name of each image on each one of them -- "School," "Cloud," "Bridge," "House," "Dog," "Car" -- as if for the first time.

Then I looked up and saw, far in the distance, San Francisco's downtown, its glittering high rises resembling a fairy-tale castle made of diamonds, with the shimmering sea dotted with sailboats as backdrop.

"City," I said, "my beautiful city." And the words rang true; they slipped into my bloodstream and suddenly I was overwhelmed by an intense hunger. I wanted to swallow the beatific landscape before me. For it was then that I intuited that, through my love for the new language, and through the act of describing and the naming of things, I, too, sounding like a hungry duck, could stake my claims in the New World.

[Andrew Lam is an editor with New America Media and the author of three books, <u>Perfume Dreams: Reflections on the Vietnamese Diaspora</u>, <u>East Eats West: Writing in Two Hemispheres</u>, and his latest, <u>Birds of Paradise Lost</u>, a collection of short stories about Vietnamese refugees struggling to rebuild their lives in the Bay Area, won the Pen Josephine Literary Awards and is a Finalist for the California Book Award 2014.]

Chapter 3: My Name is

This chapter deals with the struggles we have with our Vietnamese names.

Tên

By: Nguyen Thi Thien Phuoc

First day of school, first day of anything
I'm already hoping that you won't ask
Barely a whisper
I don't even want you to hear me
    Can you spell that?
And it's still wrong anyway
But I don't correct you
Because it's just easier that way
And there's a lump in my throat
    That's really different.
Tell me something I don't know
Blue eyes, fine hair, Rainbow Brite halloween costume
More like xôi nếp, bánh bao, and that Chinese girl's
sister
    My granddaughter is Tianna too.
There are eight different ways to spell Kaitlyn
And each has a preprinted keychain
The closest thing is the Babysitter's Club
And the Yellow Power Ranger
Never mind
    Tell me what it means.
Call me what you want
I've worn this now for many years
What my parents gave me or a version of
The badges are what matter
Refugee, immigrant, daughter, wife, mother.

Văn

By Van Dang

Văn. My name can be found carved in to the bark of a towering, aged tree in front of my home the same way it is painstakingly etched into my soul. For three decades it has stayed with me through all that I have experienced and endured, at times serving as a beacon that has guided me through turbulent, stormy waters. It was with me from the time I was a little boy, nervously setting foot into kindergarten class unable to form a coherent sentence, to the time when I graduated from the university and received my bachelor's degree. It was there when all that was true and honest within and around me escaped like a flowing stream down into what seemed like a bottomless cavern. It was there when I rose from the ashes like a rising phoenix. My name has always been, and is still is, a constant reminder of who I am. The same name was also bestowed upon my grandfather and countless of generations of Tonkin before him. In Vietnamese, a language that is known for having multiple meanings and interpretations for one word, my name is no exception. My name bears proudly its meanings — knowledge and verse.

There is an age-old belief among Vietnamese people concerning the importance of names. It's believed that names carry a powerful force that can influence a person's personality and character as they come of age. For this very reason, parents in Vietnamese culture usually take great care and caution in choosing names that reflect qualities and virtues that they wish to instill in their children. A girl who is given the name Ngọc, meaning "jade", will hopefully grow up one day to be as beautiful and resilient as the stone itself. A boy named Minh, or "bright", might possess great wisdom and intelligence. Another belief involving names is that evil spirits like to steal babies, particularly attractive ones.

62

Because of this, many parents refer to their newborns using unappealing names such as Chuột, which means "rat", or Xấu, meaning "ugly", in order to trick the spirits into staying away from them. I've come to learn that this belief and preoccupation over "evil spirits" was actually a result of very real dangers — poor hygiene, inadequate nutrition, and lack of medical attention that newborns experienced in Vietnam for decades, especially those living in rural areas, contributed to this.

At times I wondered if these centuries old beliefs are merely superstitions that were created to fend off the hardships of reality, or if my name has had a role in shaping me into the person whom I am today.

I remember lying in bed nestled against my mom's bosom the night before the first day of kindergarten. Worry festered inside of me like a swarm of hungry locusts and I struggled to fall asleep even after a round of bedtime stories. Looking up, I asked my mom in Vietnamese, "What am I going to do, school starts tomorrow…. I don't know a word of English. How am I going to communicate with the other children?" My mom whose eyes were already closed, paused for a moment, then under her breathe whispered, "Don't worry son, try your best and you'll be fine." With that said, I too closed my eyes and we both drifted away to sleep. She was right, I did do fine, and for as long as I can remember, my mom always held onto the notion that my name has helped me, that my love for writing and my insatiable desire for knowledge as always been a part of me. According to her, those Honors English and AP history classes that later appeared on my high school schedule were no coincidence. If the belief regarding names were really true, I wondered if my name could help not only myself, but others as well, that somehow, someway, my name, like two hands, could lift a person up and guide them in their struggle.

Huy

By: Huy T. Pham

It's the end of the winter term at my time at the Kellogg School of Management. And it dawns on me – none of my professors can say my name correctly.

Professor Van Mieghem calls me "Huey". Even after our lively conversation about the City of Huy in Belgium. Professor Pearlman calls me something different on a weekly basis. Professor Razeghi knows he shouldn't try. He points. That always works.

But nothing beats Professor Rogers. We spent literally 5 minutes of his first class going through my name. "Huey?" "No, Huy". "Whey?" "No, Huy." "Hai?" "Forget it. You know what? Just call me W-E. That's close enough for me." Didn't work out though – he still calls me something random.

I've gone through the exact same ritual my entire life. The first day I walk into class, I pronounce my name. I repeat it. I smile. If they get it, great. If they don't, it's okay. I don't really mind.

In fact, I've had good friends, bosses, and co-workers that have mispronounced my name for years. Usually, it catches them by surprise. Someone will point it out by saying, "Um, how do you say Huy's name?" "WEE right?" "Uh no." "What the hell? He's never corrected me. I've known that jerk for six years."

I guess I've just grown accustomed. During the first couple years of my life, I went by "Hoy" (complete with that spelling) – because I just thought that was the American pronunciation/spelling of "Huy". When I came to Kindergarten and my teacher repeated "Hoy" after I said "Huy", I just assumed I was the messed up one.

But you know what - I've never considered changing my name.

My parents went with an "H" theme – Hang, Hien, and Huy. My oldest sister went into a "name-changing" campaign in middle school. I remember that she was tired of being called "Hang 10", so she came up with a survey. Samantha won out.

Sometimes I do use a pseudonym. If you hear "Henry" at Starbucks, Fuddruckers, or Jamba Juice, turn around. It might be me.

But, otherwise, I'll always be Huy. I wear the name proudly. When you hear my name, you know I'm different. My name is a mark of my heritage, my people, and my pride. I am Vietnamese.

It's the mark of my parents. Separated by the ocean for two years. Nine months after being re-united, I was born. Scared witless about the challenges of a new land, they named me Huy. Huy means "honor", and I try to honor them with every breath I take.

Tonight, I lay in bed wondering – if my name is so important to me, why don't I care when people mispronounce it? Did I just give up?

And, I realize, no that's not it. It's something deeper than that. My parents (Cuc and Dung*) don't speak English very well. But they are very well-loved by their co-workers and neighbors. And they taught me something very important.

A name is just something people call you by. People might not necessarily remember your name or how to say it. They might not even remember the words you say. But you know what they never forget? How you make them *feel*.

You make your name by *who you are.*

[One last funny story about the name "Huy." At an exit interview for my last job, my Russian boss told the HR Director that I must be leaving the company because he kept calling me "male genitalia." The HR Director was shocked. Apparently "Huy" is slang for male genitalia in Russian, to which my Russian boss told me – hey, at least the gender is right.

I told this story to my father, who had no sympathy for me. My father, Dung, has his own name issues. "My name means feces and the other shop workers made fun of me, so I added a z. They couldn't say Dzung, so I went with my saint name, and now they laugh that my initials mean urine." - Dung "Dzung" Peter Pham aka Dad on 30 years of name problems.]

What's in a name?

Vietnamese identity in three vignettes.

By: Madeleine Yen Vu

Little bird emerging.

I think when I was about ten, flipping through a Merriam-Webster, I found out that my name existed in the English dictionary. I knew that it was a type of bird in Vietnamese and also that it was a currency used in Japan, but to find it legitimized in an official publication was cooler than any Jessica, Amanda, or Erin I ever wished to be. "Yen, noun, a strong desire for something or to do something." Bragging rights secured, in the obscure occasions when the topic of names would come up, I would boast sophomorically, "Yen actually has three definitions" saving my dictionary definition for last.

Then one day, while flipping through the 7 or so local television channels I had access to growing up, I came across a PBS special that featured cave swiftlets. These were special Southeast Asian birds that dwelled in caves and used saliva to build their nests. These nests were difficult to attain but were sought after because they had unique culinary value. In a similar Eureka-esque moment as before, I realized, this was the chim yến! That was me! I was a swiftlet! Learning the term for yến this time around was even better than discovering that my name existed in a dictionary. Now I could explain that not only was I a bird, I was a valuable and unique kind of bird. My parents naming me after a bird wasn't so tacky of a story. As if I needed more reason to talk about myself as a teenager, not only could I mention my legitimacy in the English language, I could even embellish the fact with a cultural element. Bragging rights doubly secured, for better or for worse.

As interesting as it might sound, to have my parents name me after a rare and valuable species, the truth is that they chose yến as a name because I was a small baby at birth, as small as a bird. Only after many years, as a vagabond young adult did this prove to be an appropriate name choice. The phone calls home, from distant institutions or distant countries, realized the image of a far away daughter, ultimately manifesting the meaning of the fleeting bird.

Father, reluctantly letting go of his bird.

Silly at heart, genuine to the bone, he is serious when matters demand his seriousness. Oh, and he is never on time, he is always early. His behavior is an accurate reflection of his character. He will tell you like it is as he has told the women in his life: "that man is not for you," "I think you should keep on that weight," "your fish is too salty." He has but his experiences to found his wisdom, yet his intelligence is refined and his intuition uncanny.

Here he is, a man who is approaching his 7th decade of life, the wisest person I know and have access to, telling me in this fortune session: "you have a tendency to move around, never staying in one place."

If fortune telling is an ambiguous rephrasing of the present, then my dad definitely has it mastered. "Uh dad, can you tell me something I don't know?" I respond distrustingly.

But thankfully, because I'm prompted to read between the lines, he doesn't have to, explicitly.

In acknowledging my fleeting nature, he has compromised his fatherly tendency toward control over to every other force that may take his daughter away. He has humbled himself to let me know he loves me, believes in me, respects me, all enough to let me go. Of course, still trusting, hoping, that I will always come back.

I didn't think it was possible to both love and lament at the same time, for time is something that we cannot seize for ourselves. Time in the form of age, for example, can be brutal and comforting. Despite our generational gap, it seems that we have both been subject to the same violence that Time thrusts upon us: his age, my age; his immobility, my vagabondage.

If my father had been able to cope with it, I hope to learn to be able to do it too. But he's so much better at it than I will ever be.

I like to think it comes with age.

Little bird soars, inevitably.

Sitting in my first day of Vietnamese class, Thầy explains to the entire class that Vietnamese names are unique because they all have meanings. While he is interpreting his own, I contemplate mine: Bảo Yến …Bảo as in to protect or preserve, Yến as in the little swiftlet.

The Vietnamese tradition in naming a child is surrounded with superstition, never arbitrary. Sometimes, the names brought nostalgia of the past, and sometimes were like predictions, or rather, projections of the future. While some captured sentiments and perceptions, others captured hopes and dreams, and if the parents were lucky, these hopes were manifested for their children.

A first encounter with a Vietnamese name could tell so much about the person, where she was from, what kind of family she grew up in, and maybe even the fate of her future. But rather than acknowledging these intricacies in a name, we often dismiss them as superstitious titles, claiming that we should never judge a book by its cover.

Perhaps naming me Bảo Yến was a gentle gesture to keep me sheltered and protected, but if my vagabond nature and unsettled lifestyle after turning 18 was a contradiction to their original intentions, my parents have been nothing but supportive. I hope they don't consider themselves unlucky because their "hope" in a name didn't exactly turn out as they expected. Rather, I hope they find themselves proud, without regret, for letting me finally make my own decisions. Because even if I am not or no longer their secured precious chim yến, my name is an ever-present reminder of my Vietnamese identity. And I am reminded every day that I have a safe haven nearby regardless of the distance, a home that is yearning for my return, a place that boasts my Vietnamese roots.

Nha Trang

By: Trang Nguyen

In my life, I have been known by three names. Before University, I was known by one name, in University, I asked to be called another, and after that, I changed it again. Three times my name has changed and yet it remained the same.

My name is Trang, or more precisely, Nha Trang. I was named after my parents' hometown, in memory of all that they had left behind. Loaded with meaning and place, it is a good name, but Nha and Trang do not translate well into English. Nha becomes "nah" and Trang starts like train but ends like clang. My light and pretty name is instead an awkward clash of heavy jarring sounds.

As I child I knew no better and allowed myself to be called Nah Trrr-ang. We were refugees who were simply grateful for the chance at a better future, with bigger problems to tackle than the pronunciation of names. Ignoring the trauma of war and communism, we were all too busy trying to survive in this foreign world and support our families left behind in Vietnam. But as time passed it started to bother me. At home I was Trang, but as soon as I left the house my name would morph into some strange other sound to which I would also respond.

For years I lived in dread of anything to do with my name. I would tense through the start of the school year when the teacher would struggle with bewilderment through all of our Vietnamese names. I would hesitate when introducing myself, getting caught between saying my name as it is meant to be said and what it had become, before begrudgingly mumbling out the anglicised bastardisation.

My story is not unique and many other Vietnamese people have resolved the problem by changing their names. Hân has become Therese; Hải to Kevin; and Huy to Damian. But I didn't want a new name; I just wanted to be called as I was named.

By the time I reached University, an entire generation of Vietnamese children had either taken an English name or given their names over to bastardisations with little resistance. With time, I became resigned to things, but the "Nah" grated on me. Given that I was rarely ever called my full name, I began introducing myself as simply Trr-ang.

I didn't think things would ever change and yet it did. After University, I volunteered for nine months in VOICE's office in the Philippines working with and helping to resettle stateless Vietnamese people who had no trouble pronouncing my name. The turning point was when I began being introduced to non-Vietnamese people as Trang. For years I had agonised and hesitated whenever I had to introduce myself, but here I was, being introduced as Trang without a second thought. Foreigners would struggle with my name, but they would get there in the end. I was thunderstruck and wondered why did I ever think it was so hard?

Several years have passed now, and my world has expanded many times over but I am still resolutely Trang. I don't baulk at the blank looks I get sometimes when I introduce myself and calmly repeat my name until it is understood. People still get confused over how my name sounds nothing like the way it looks, but I am patient and explain that this is how you say my name. I explain that there is nothing like the Vietnamese 'tr' sound in English, that it is closer to a 'jr' sound than anything else, and that the 'ng' in my name is like that in sing. If they ask about my full name, I will even explain that the 'nh' is like the Spanish ñ. Sometimes, I meet

Vietnamese people and their eyes widen when they realise what I've done.

It took me over 25 years to find the courage to speak up for myself, but I've learnt that if I don't, no one else will. No one will ever understand and appreciate the nuances of the Vietnamese language and Vietnamese names, and things will never change. My name is Trang, and I am asking you to say it as it is. I am Vietnamese: this is who I am.

[Nha Trang is a resident of Australia. We forgive our Australian sister for her use of "s" where we prefer to use "z".]

Chapter 4: Family

(Huy T. Pham's hip family gathered at his baptism.)

This chapter deals with the bonds and reverence we have with our families.

Mai Quynh's Story

By: Mai Quynh

I must have been about ten years old when I first
considered the idea that my father might actually carry
on a whole life when he wasn't at home, taking care of
me. This, as a child, is something you simply don't
conceive. You see a world that is custom fit and built for
your eyes only. People are always playing with you.
Feeding you. Clothing you. You're everyone's focus
and envy. And everything just feels easy and free. But
then, a handful of years pass and you slowly understand
the machine behind the curtain. And my parents,
honest hard-working Vietnamese immigrants, masked
the machine well.

I must have been about ten years old when I first asked
my father, "ba, what do you do?" Well, it occurred to me
that ba wasn't at home all day. My mom, on the other
hand, had her hands full around the clock suffering my
every last fuss, scream and whimper.

My ba told me what he did. He spent his days screwing
caps on toothpaste bottles. Oh, the little things. I'd be
remiss if I didn't add a small wrinkle: he was also putting
himself through college to become an engineer.
Working by day, studying by night. His life was the stuff
of fiction. It turns out he'd endured numerous odd-jobs
toiling away at menial places to pave his way to a better
life. This is how he spent countless hours every day.
And his story was a success. He eventually earned his
stripes as a computer engineer. It amazes me to this
day.

My mom somehow managed to juggle the needs of
three children, while at the same time spending her days
nursing others at a convalescent home to provide for the
family financially. She was tough as nails. When
nursing became too taxing on her time at home, she

became a freelance seamstress and worked out of the house. All while cooking, cleaning and picking up after three rowdy children. It worked out for me just as well. More time for her to cook me the best "cá kho tộ" and "canh chua cá" this side of Vietnam. She was a spectacular cook, and I don't say that lightly. Thanks to her amazing talent, my nose still perks up to this day at the smell of Vietnamese spices simmering in the distance.

I wasn't the easiest child to deal with. I was a bit of a trouble maker. I'd graduated high school with little direction and little ambition. I wanted to be a success, but I didn't know where to look. And the traditional college route was decidedly not for me. So, I bought some time and waited on tables.

But things forever changed the day my father tragically passed away. I was 21. And he was only 50. I was devastated. There is nothing more sobering in this world than the death of a loved one. But, as the tears dried and the smoke cleared, I reflected on my father's memory and all that he stood for. And I determined that the best way to honor his memory, and honor the uniquely wonderful upbringing my parents had provided me, was to carry on my life as they had carried on theirs. It was there and then that I decided to become a makeup artist.

And, as it turned out, my story in many ways paralleled theirs. It's no coincidence. They set the standards by which I conduct my life. They were my role models. I, too, started my career at the bottom of the totem pole. I had little experience and fewer prospects. But, I was determined to be a makeup artist. And I was determined to be a success. I suffered naysayers, obstacles and various challenges along the way. I attended beauty school. Worked behind a makeup counter. Assisted the assistant on amateur photo shoots and videos. It wasn't always easy, and it wasn't a road paved in gold. But, I stayed the course, and the rest is history.

My father was an engineer. My mother, a homemaker, a nurse, a seamstress. They arrived in the states independently and with very little, until their stars crossed in California and they decided to build a home together. Neither spoke any more than a handful of words of broken English when they arrived. Neither had gone to college. They didn't have a big network of friends or family nearby. But, somehow they managed to push forward and provide me and my sisters with a life so many others take for granted. Sadly, they've both passed away. But they live on, not only in memory, but in me.

It wasn't, as I thought as a young child, easy and free. It was hard work. It was focus. It was blood, sweat, tears, and love. It is these principles to which I owe all of my success.

… and maybe, just maybe, one of these days I'll find a "cá kho tộ" and "canh chua cá" that comes even close to rivaling my mother's.

[Mai Quynh is a leading celebrity makeup artist with over 16 years of professional experience. Mai's distinctive approach has also captured the attention of world-renowned fashion magazines like Vogue, Harper's Bazaar, Elle, Marie Claire and Blackbook. Mai's relentless devotion to her craft and her unremitting desire for perfection continues to this day, cementing her status as one of Hollywood's top makeup artists.]

Mythical Parentals

By: Huy T. Pham

When I was younger, I didn't need role models and superheroes. I had mom and dad. Dad with his supernatural willpower, working long hours at sea as a commercial fisherman. Mom with her optimistic outlook, raising her three children basically as a single parent. Language and cultural barriers be damned, nothing could stop my mythical parentals.

But, as I grew older, my parents became less mythical and more real. My heroes developed personalities. I began to see quirks and cracks in my idealistic personifications. I began to wonder if I was adopted.

My mother is a hoot. When I told her I was graduating at the top of my class, she hit me upside my head and told me to stop lying. That is my mommy.

She once asked me at dinner what I thought about heart transplants. She wanted to know whether or not she would still love the people she did if she gave her heart away. Cute, I know... but damn. I freaking lost it. My dad and I couldn't stop laughing through dinner.

My dad is a teaser - I get it from him. He calls my mom "country". And it's hard to argue when she's addicted to pro wrestling. My family dinners aren't typical. Last Friday we ate our Lenten fish while watching the retirement of Edge from WWF. It was big news for her.

She's diabetic, so I've been trying to get her to eat healthy. She knows I watch her, so sometimes she hides her cookies and eats them alone.

I've been trying to get her to exercise. Instead, she buys this new Vietnamese machine that shakes her body while she lays down. I'm pretty sure I could build one of these things at 1/5 the price with a vacuum cleaner and some bolts. I try to explain to her what I think, but unfortunately she believes the Vietnamese advertising more than her own son.

It's cool though. This thing shakes her body so hard her shoulder hurts. I ask if she has lost any weight. Nope, gained 2lbs, and now my shoulder hurts, she says. I ask if she's going to stop using it. She says no, I got to keep trying. I see her lay down and turn on the machine again, this time holding an ice pack against her shoulder. I shit you not. Perseverance.

A few months ago, she backed into our neighbor's car. It was pretty obvious; the car was behind us in the driveway. I hear the doorbell ring. My mom shouts down the stairwell, "They have no proof! Tell them I didn't do it!" No joke.

My dad? Conspiracy theorist at its best. I can't even watch a football game without him accusing Vegas of controlling everything.

My father loves watching the Spanish channel. Now I understand why. If you're not going to understand the TV anyways, you might as well watch pretty women. Genius.

I gave him a Kellogg sweatshirt for Christmas. He thanked me for giving him one of those free shirts you got with cereal. He had no idea where I went to school.

The sweatshirt would go well with my father's French pumps. They got like 2 inches on the side. I borrowed them once for a debate tournament and got so much shit for wearing my father's heels.

Yeahh...Mom and Dad? Not so much superheroes any more.

But their love is truly unconditional.

Let me illustrate. I hate going to the doctor's. We didn't have insurance growing up, so I always feel like I can walk it off. Plus, I hate constructive criticism. Pay a doctor to tell me what's wrong? Please. Ignorance is bliss.

I have eczema on my arms that likes to flare up during the winter. My parents tell me to go talk to a doctor. I refuse.

A care package arrives with a bunch of creams. I don't trust Vietnamese medicine. I grew up taking medication from God knows who, prescribed for God knows what. So, I googled. Turns out one of the creams is for gonorrhea. I called my mom to ask her WTF.

My sister explains to me later that because I refused to go to the doctor, my mom told my dad to go to the dermatologist and ask the dermatologist what he should do if he "theoretically" had eczema that flares up during the winter. I am not sure how that became gonorrhea cream, but alright.

No doubt, my parents are crazy, but in an endearing kind of way.

As they become less mythical, and I've become more self-sufficient, I do find that I treat them differently. They've become less like parents and more like old friends.

I tend to tease my mom a lot, usually with my father's help. I like to physically push my mom out of the way. When she complains about me, I threaten to send her to a retirement home. Today, when she was showing me her medical bills, I straight-faced told her that I was tired of her getting sick. That she needed to stop it. I think she knows we're kidding. I certainly hope so.

I do need to change my behavior a little bit though. I was recently in my best friend's nursery. I saw Shel Silverstein's _The Giving Tree_ on the bookshelf.

Two decades later, I finally got the point.

The tree exists to give to the boy unconditionally. Like a parent, despite getting nothing in return, the tree puts the boy's needs first. The tree is sad when it feels it has nothing left to give the boy and that the boy might never return.

I understand why my parents still like to help me move, change my oil and do my laundry, despite my (not so serious) protest. Although I am (pretty) self-sufficient, they still want to give.

They still want to be superheroes. Cute.

Well, they got it. I'll continue to make them feel needed. After all my mythical parentals have done, the least I owe them is a bit of illusion.

Realization

By: Richie Le

I remember the first time my mom dropped me off at Viet
school
I dreaded the next hours of teaching I had to sit through
Not in tuned with the benefits, and neither the culture
All I wanted to do was tell my parents which sport I could
go for
I was thinking basketball, shoot hoops and pass
But next thing I knew, I was stuck in a Vovinam class
While the other kids spoke Viet and I didn't relate too
well
'Cause they were different than my friends I hung out
with K through 12
So it seemed I failed all these Viet qualifications
But at school I got told, "oh my gosh you're like my
favorite Asian!"
So isn't that good enough? Well at least it seemed
Until you come to realize what it honestly means
To represent the upbringing your parents tried to give
you
The struggles of the war and bullshit they went through
The long months they had to sit through for hopes of a
better life
Cramped in small boats with loads of dirty mice
With no real advice how to make it to the promise land
Some would say they got dealt with an awful hand
But to flip what they had and come out victorious
Just shows the struggle and how great my parents story
is
Or better yet, maybe even your parents too
Cause sometimes it takes walking in someone else's
pair of shoes
So from the Vovinam class and the language they
wanted me to speak
I finally realize what my parents were trying to teach!

[Richie is a spoken word artist, focusing on trying to continue the Vietnamese culture in ways kids understand and relate to. Check out his site at www.youtube.com/RICHIELE23.]

I'm a Pham…

By: Huy T. Pham

The other day I was talking to one of my law school boys about Thanksgiving. The topic turned to whether or not I was going to go home for the holidays. I vacillated a bit. I had finals to study for. The travel days for Thanksgiving basically suck. You come home and you're back in a flash. But, I've always flown home for every Thanksgiving. Sadly, I guess I find less and less reason to come home.

I was telling my boy this when he stopped, shook his head and said, "WHAT? Don't you like, love your family? Don't they, like, love you?"

Awww I know you didn't. Don't you be going there. Don't be talking about my family. I tell you what I am. I'm a Pham. Get it right.

Phams don't hug. I'm not sure if I've ever hugged my mom or my dad. Even when I graduated high school. Or left for college. Or left for law school

Phams don't call. Unless I'm coming home and need someone to pick me up from the airport. Then, well, maybe…

Phams don't keep pictures of one another. I swear only like three of you know what my two sisters and my parents look like.

Phams don't share. Heck if my parents ever knew I ever dated anyone. Or the name of my closest friends.

I'm not saying we're perfect. When I get my own kids (let's concentrate on finding a girlfriend first, Huy…), I'm certainly going to hug them. I'm undecided on the whole sharing or calling bit yet… That's a little… not masculine...

But I'll tell you what Phams are.

Phams understand that love is unconditional. You grow up with a fisherman father and a seamstress mother that worked long hours... and offshore... to the point where you never really got to know them... that's when you understand what true love is.

Phams understand the worth of every single human being. My parents would whoop my ass if I ever disrespected another human being. You may be smarter than some. Taller than some (dubious). Better at basketball. But you're never better. Just different.

Phams love their friends as their family. That's just how we roll. We never had a big family growing up (result of the post war migration), so we made our own. Friends. Family. Same difference.

Phams give everything they have, no matter what it is. It could be peeling shrimp in the driveway at 3am. Doesn't matter. Be the best damn shrimp peeler you can.

That's what we are. We are Phams.

We may not be built to say "I Love You" or to express how we feel about one another. But we know.

I don't need to come home for Thanksgiving, or to call regularly, or to share my life to tell my parents how much I love them. I do that by being the person they taught me to be. A Pham.

Nothing could make them prouder.

And when I finally find a woman to have beautiful babies with, I'll print this out and paste it on my children's walls. Kids, remember what it means to be a Pham. Now, give your pansy father a hug.

A Note in a Song

By: Sydney Nguyen

As a young girl, I remember my parents working hard to support our family even though it was rough. All seven of us stayed in a shabby, one-bedroom apartment, and the restroom often had problems and overflowed. I remember one Christmas when one of my older sisters counted out a hundred pennies from her sock-bag to buy me a big lollipop. This memory is bittersweet for me. It reminds me of how much my sister loves me but also how poor we were. Another memory that will always remain with me is how I used to count out forty cents from my mini M&M container each morning. Forty cents was precious to me, since it was enough to pay for my free and reduced lunch in kindergarten.

Unfortunately, pennies would not be enough for college or other areas of life, and free and reduced things are hard to come by. Given that my dad did not attend college and my mom only attended school up to the sixth grade, it is not surprising that my path to college was an uphill battle. I entered high school with the mentality that I must work hard. I was salutatorian of my class of 600 students while juggling extracurricular activities such as NHS, Orchestra, and several sports. My involvement and rank opened up an array of scholarship opportunities for me. Hoping to secure a full scholarship, I applied for many of them. I wanted to experience college without counting the pennies and focus on learning. Proudly, I achieved my goal of financing my double degree in Political Science and Spanish without burdening my parents.

While I am proud of my achievement, I do believe that my experience has a familiar ring, as a note in song does. What immigrant families seem to all have in common is the perseverance to overcome adversity and the value of family. The achievements that we accomplish serve as lessons to teach us to stay positive and approach problems from a solution point of view, and the sacrifices our parents make remind us to be forever grateful to have family.

Chapter 5: Mothers

[Author Viet Hoai Tran carrying his mother at his graduation.]

This chapter covers the special relationship we have with our Vietnamese mothers. Our mothers are generally the strong, resilient pillar in our families.

My Turn to Carry you

By Viet Hoai Tran

My mother's departure from Vietnam could be best explained as casting a Vietnamese novel that is aged, with pages torn, but still rich in breadth into the sea. Her arrival in the United States was opening a new book – mint condition, with that fresh new smell, and pages still crisp at the touch. The words – the language is unrecognizable, but the first chapter is the name of the infant she carried over: Tran Hoai Viet. She holds this new book dear to her heart, and has bright hope for this new beginning that is her and her son's new life.

My mother has held various positions and jobs throughout her time in the United States. The will of such an individual is unceasing and it's amazing in what she has done and still continues to do. Here are a few of the "titles" she has taken. She was the girl that grew up among a group of seven boys. She was the child that walked miles to attend the nearest public school. She was the single daughter that received the highest education. She was the female professional that held the most respected position in her field. She was the educator that persevered through a war-torn country. She was the widow that faced austerity to leave her own country. She was the immigrant carrying an infant son to live in a compacted home. She was the silent American muted by her poor English skills. She was the diligent baker, seamstress, babysitter, to meet day's end. She was the parent to say goodbye to her son on the first day of preschool, but the first standing at the gate to pick him up. She was the avid reader at the library who checked out book titles such as "How To Write In Cursive", "Geometry 101", and "Science Projects for Beginners." She was the worst tennis enthusiast, but the biggest fan of one of the team's star players. She was the make-up artist, the photographer, and the videographer at her son's graduation. She was the technologist that searched on Google, "how much college cost," "jobs in San Diego," and "what is financial aid?" She was the insomniac that stayed up until 3AM with her son because he had a final tomorrow and offered "I make coffee for you? How about some fried rice? Anything you want." But lastly, the role she held the best - is being a mother.

All mothers are incredible beings. They have served different positions, taken various jobs, assumed unconventional roles – all for the purpose of nurturing the ones they love.

Who would have thought that roughly 20 years ago, an educator, widow, a sister- a mother, carried a young infant with arms as feeble and a heart as broken as the war-torn country she called home for four decades? She brought him to a place where she had the greatest conviction and the brightest of hopes he would have opportunities unlike anywhere else in the world. She named me, Tran Hoai Viet, "Always Vietnam", to remember her homeland but to remember the very reasons she left as well.

It was one June 15th, 2014, the day of my graduation from UCSD that I could proudly say: "Mẹ, it's my turn to carry you."

I have carried you through my studies. While many immigrants and first generation students feel that they have expectations to fulfill - that weight and "burden" should not bring you down. It should be the anchor that holds you and reminds you of your roots. Where you come from and who you are should not confine you to what you should do or who you should be - but rather be the shining beacon leading you to your greatest potential.

I realize that my mother is that beacon. From high school through college, I find myself in the most abysmal of places. But she served as the light that illuminated the very pathway I've been elusive to take. If you leave the grandest of sailboats landlocked, you'll never see its fullest potential scaling the waves of the high seas.

At graduation, I proceeded down the aisle heading towards our assigned seats. I remember my mother telling me that she sat at the very front. As I continued, I waited and waited to see her face. The line of proud parents and smiling strangers stretched but I didn't see my mother's face yet. Finally, I see a glimpse of her – a purple shade she wears only on special occasion in memory of my deceased father. We were all here together on this momentous occasion. I see the light that is her face and a wave of emotions overcoming me. This is the light she must have seen when she got off the plane to a new country. One filled with the promise of opportunity and freedom. I quickly planted a kiss on her check, wiped the tear from my eye and caught up with the line.

Later, as I proceeded on stage to receive the Dean's Award for Leadership and Service, the Dean read a piece from my most recent and last published journal article – quoting from the part in which I dedicated to my mother.

"She is the diamond among the crowd of people as you walk across the stage for your college diploma – you are smiling and she is crying."

Everyone told me I was beaming on stage, with a smile that runs deeper than grandest of canyons. As I walked back to my seat, I get a text from my brother: "Mom was crying the whole time you were up there but with the biggest smile on her face."

This one is for you, Mẹ. My accomplishments, my awards, my graduation are for you. You have made this possible. It's my turn to carry you from now on. I tell the story of this courageous, headstrong woman because when doing so, it reveals who I am. This is my mother's story, but soon it will become mine.

Cảm ơn mẹ, con thương mẹ rất nhiều.

To my mother, Tran Thi Minhtam.

See, Smell, Taste, Hear, Feel

By: Hung T. Pham

Can you see that she sells her labor to you,
her dignity
through English that she knows through phrasebooks,
English that,
in kindergarten,
I knew better than her?

When my mother limps through the door at night
after her daily twelve hours
of painting unfamiliar nails and
pampering exhausted feet that are
ironically
not her own,
she whimpers in embarrassment sometimes
and anger, others,
when customers shout at her and say things exactly like
"don't talk to me in Asian"
but mom,
mẹ đẹp tuyệt vời.

Can you smell the acetone in the nail salon that floods
her with
cancerous free radicals that
motivate her to sing songs of me in her head as she
uses her hands every day to
beautify you instead of her
and
constantly remind herself that she can't afford the very
services
she paints on your body?

Strong like the heart that I see before I touch her skin,
wise like the lioness who makes her home strong like
steel
from within

its walls,
she manufactures short friendships in the salon to
mass produce meager change,
so that I can change
what God has put her through
to give me
the blessings in exchange
and mom,
mẹ đẹp tuyệt vời.

Can you taste the white rice and smelly fish that she
eats,
on her break (singular),
the only things
that she eats
that you complain about
that reek of Vietnam in the shop
that,
because she is anemic,
must eat to continue working to keep me from
smelling
of how she smelled like growing up,
of how that fish smells like,
of how putrid your ignorance smells like?

Try swallowing the biotin pills for her falling hair,
bitter
like the nonexistent grudges my
mother holds against those customers who
stole her purse behind the counter that one time,
because she would rather worry about me
than them
and mom,
mẹ đẹp tuyệt vời.

Can you hear her laugh so loud at the dinner table
because we are happy
because we are rich
because

wealth is measured by how much you have in your heart
and
not in your pocket?

But, I hate the way she covers up her smile because
she has crowns that she thinks are too ugly,
that one day she'll be able to wear on her head and
that when she looks in the mirror
it won't have to hurt anymore as I
stab the insecurities dead
with the sharpness of my academic success
and mom,
mẹ đẹp tuyệt vời.

Can you feel the soreness in her lower back as she
remains bent double for hours as she
scrubs away at your filthy soles
but also at her soul
too humble for her to even recognize
how worthy she is of something greater than
how you treat her?

Don't you fucking dare talk to my angel mother like that,
who often returns home in tears because of things
exactly like
"don't talk to me in Asian"
because
karma knows everyone's address
and mom,
mẹ đẹp tuyệt vời.

Mom, mẹ đẹp tuyệt vời.
Mom, mẹ đẹp tuyệt vời.
Mom, mẹ đẹp tuyệt vời.
Mom, mẹ đẹp tuyệt vời.
Mom, mẹ đẹp tuyệt vời.

Happy Birthday Momma

By: Anhlan Nguyen

Dearest Mommy,

Today marks a very special day for you as we celebrate your 79th birthday! I was planning to write this note much earlier, but a hectic day at work prevented me to collect enough thoughts to write and I do want to write something special to honor you mother! You dedicated most of your life to a teaching career that impacted thousands of students in Vietnam. Since you started your teaching career at a very early age (19), you spent more than 30 years teaching high school mathematics at the Trung Vuong high school and you taught us well.

I cannot be thankful enough for all of your lessons of disciplines and hard work when we were very young since they stayed with me all of my life. When Dad left the country to search for freedom after being imprisoned in re-education camp, you took the role of both a mother and a father to take care of all of us. You did such a fine job raising all of us until the day we were reunited in Canada.

Arriving in Canada in your middle ages, you once again taught us the values of discipline and determination. I still remember seeing you getting up very early in the morning around 3:00am to recite the lessons in English as you came back to school for some Professional Certificate to allow you to get a better job. You did not want us to see your effort to memorize words and reading out loud, so you got up really early to finish all the study when we were still asleep. I still remember your beautiful smile on the Graduation day as you finished your study. I was so proud of you, mommy!

Words cannot express how much love and appreciation I have for you. Lately I have been thinking about the journey you have left on this earth. I know that you are in the painful process of exiting this world and it's truly heart breaking to see you suffering from chronic pain every day. Being diagnosed with both Dementia and having spinal stenosis, the past three years have been truly challenging for all of us to witness your withering health condition. I cannot imagine how I would handle this chronic pain if it were me… but if I could exchange years of my life for your well-being, I would be so happy to do it mommy!

So Mother, on your birthday, I want to send you my best wishes for a beautiful birthday celebration and a new year that is full of Peace, Love and Healing… May Buddha bless you with the inner peace to overcome the pain. May you be blessed with all the love from dad, your children and everyone around you.

Happy Birthday with all of my love!

Your daughter,

Anhlan Nguyen

[Chi Anhlan is a dear friend of and mentor of mine. Anhlan served as president of the Vietnamese Culture and Science Association from 1999-2004, and has served as the Chair of the Board since then. She has received numerous awards for her dedication to community service and was appointed to the Board of Directors of the Vietnam Education Foundation by President Obama in 2012.]

My Superhero

By: Katherine Tran

I told my mother I loved her for the first time when I was 16. As expected, she responded with, "What do you want?" That basically sums up my family when it comes to emotional expressions. Love is something you show through actions, not words. If I had expected verbal affirmation, I would've been sorely disappointed.

My family didn't have much when I was growing up. Back to school shopping at the Salvation Army was the norm, and toys were a luxury. Second-hand goods were the way of life for us. I was proud and happy to wear my "new" $2 jeans on the first day of school. I looked forward to Christmas every year when I would receive a brand new dress from a fancy department store. Keeping up with the Jones wasn't part of my lifestyle.

Although we didn't have cable TV or other forms of entertainment my peers had, I never felt deprived. My childhood was rich with love and family time. My mother spent her days studying English while working a full time job to provide for us; she was my superhero. Her bedtime stories consisted of stories of Vietnam - the joys and struggles of life. She reminded her children of sacrifices others made for us so that we could get to where we were. She was a strict disciplinarian who also spoiled her children in small ways. One day in elementary school, I came home and told my mother I'd rather eat sloppy joes than thịt kho. She immediately pulled out a recipe book and made sloppy joes. (For the record, thịt kho tastes better.) Instead of resting after a long day of work, my mother spent her evenings hemming dresses and jeans to fit her height-challenged daughters. She cooked new dishes every meal for us while eating leftovers herself. My mother's entire focus was on us, her family.

Somewhere along the way, I forgot about my mother's love and sacrifice. A demanding job and busy social life took precedence over the woman who had given me so much, the first person whom I confessed my love to. As I get older, I yearn to go back to the past when life was simpler. After spending so much time purposely moving away from my mother, I now find comfort in resting my head on her shoulder to feel her close. I yearn for the days when I was small enough to sit on her lap to listen to the stories of her youth. I want to make her feel special and loved, the way she made me feel when I was little. I want to go back to the days of hearing "You can do better" after showing her a report card with straight A's – it was her way of saying she knew I could push myself further. I want to go back to the days where love can be felt, where words needn't be said, and my mother, my superhero, is but an arm's length away.

My Mother's Hands

By: Jennifer Nguyen

What does Vietnam mean? Dive into any American history textbook; our country equates to three pages of war. Go into a kitchen and ask any chef; our country is a bowl of steamy beef noodle. Go up to a male stranger; our country is beautiful long haired girls in Áo dài. Approach any college student on a Thursday; our people can hold down their alcohol. Since birth, my ideology of Vietnam was manifested by people's description of its history: a country fabricated in both the bloodshed of war and the beauty of its shoreline. Yet here I sit contemplating this very question for weeks — what does Vietnam mean to me? To provide one sentence is injustice and to call it home is too typical. I finally came to a conclusion: Vietnam— a country of 128,565 square miles nurturing over 89 million people — equates to two hands. Not just any hands. If you look pass the fragile skin, shriveled fingers, and tender touches, these hands wield power. Chemically damaged and severely scarred, these hands hold the power to strike fear into my heart, yet mold and nurture me as well. To me, my country equates to my mother's hands.

Heuristically, my country is microscopic on the world's map, but with its name comes headline stories of great disdain. Ruled, dictated, and branded, my country's history makes it seem crippled and hopeless. Though beautiful in nature with scenery that can leave one breathless, no beauty can paint over its bloody history. To the world, Vietnam is branded with cannons, gunshots, torturous traps, and the bloodshed blanketing its land. Likewise, hands fatigued from twelve-hour workdays, swollen knuckles, and palms callous and cracked. The only language my mother's hands speak is that of hardship and labor. For just a couple of dimes and dollars, these hands willingly embrace the strong acidic chemicals that deteriorate its skin and maneuver blades sharp enough to leave damaging scars. When this small middle-aged lady looks at her hand, she thinks, "All of this abuse and deprivation will be okay, just as long as it will ensure one thing: my daughters' hands will not resemble mine." My mother's tough skin resembles my country, for even when it is marked and burned, it demonstrates perseverance. It survives and creates new beginnings. Like my mother, Vietnam took the unfair deck it was dealt, and synthesizes these setbacks into something that will liberate it from its history — a painted picture of new beginnings.

Shed away this skin and remove the mask of war and bloodshed; beneath its cover, Vietnam holds the perfect materials to create powerful warriors. The muscle in my mother's hands has been actively working since the age of six. Though rigid and weak, small and broken, these hands are strong. These hands understand rules and structure; they can cause physical harm to teach me, yet ache to the core when it is given. When I am scared, these hands can form tightly wound fists that will fight and protect. As time progresses, these hands are an assurance and they do not know how to let go. When the insanity of the world takes all that I have and I get to that point where I am barely held together with scotch tape and spit, these hands are my anchors. It has nurtured me and has continually raised me. After forty years, those six year old hands have single-handedly raised three: a doctor, a counselor, and a writer. How does this relate to Vietnam? Pummeled with the disadvantages of war, its people aspired for freedom. With barely five words of English and hope for a better future, they step foot into what will be the darkest of path to obtaining that future. With that, Vietnam created warriors. Warriors that were battered by the ocean's wave, beaten and raped by soulless pirates, and murdered by starvation and the saltiness of the dry ocean this went on for days, weeks, months. Tired, broken, and exhausted eyes flooded with visions of death, with the promise of another day or a vision of land can never be guaranteed. In the midst of this treachery, these warriors found hope. They embraced and transformed this hope to surviving another day. Like my mother's hands created and raised three warriors, my country created millions. For the millions of warriors that have had the grace and bravery to survive the treacherous path to America, they now have a new task. They are embodied as the representation of Vietnam; a clean slate from the stigmatism of war, and my mother was one.

Take away the war and its people and you are left with its tradition and history. It was a new beginning for these warriors. Once they step foot on this land, they were given hope and freedom. Those ideologies could only go so far when its people are empty-handed. They have nothing but the very label of being a Vietnamese refuge; no money, no job, no home, no language. With two words of English, one warrior went door to door offering to iron clothing each day, every day. That $20 she brought home was the sole source of survival for her husband and their one year old daughter. Twenty years later, my mother is still working. Hands, beaten and battered. The blood that keeps her hands working was the exact blood that symbolizes my origin. The blood that fed three and loved four. When my mother is gone, I no longer have that physical safe haven of her hands to nurture and protect me. When she leaves this world, my mom will leave behind three things: charitable acts of love, great nails, and her kids. For the same blood that runs through her hands also run through mine. In the end, my country is me. I reflect my country, I mirror it, and I demonstrate it. I am Vietnam. It is my responsibility to utilize my two hands to pass on her teachings.

The blood that flows in the veins of hundreds of millions of people all over the world is the very same one that flows through mine, and it traces back to a small pixel on a map. The stories of its war, its refuge, a mother's nurture, and a father's sacrifices — all are depicted within the very blood that is in my hands. The tradition and culture I was raised in is the basis of my morals. My mother had millions of lessons, verbal and physical. There is one lesson she has taught me that stands out, and that is the basis of this essay: to keep your palms open and to refuse no one. My mother's hands were open to receive everything the world had to offer including the pain, joy, dreams, and disappointments. They hug, they hold, they shared. They shared life stories like books. You read the tales of heartache, of hopes, and roads untaken in the lines of the palms. Fingers like chapters and memories, waiting to be unfurled. These hands are finite and know no limits. For when you hold them in a fist, it is hard to open. When you press your palm against someone else's, you create a story. You share and pass on your culture and lineage through your actions.

What does my country mean to me? It means my mother's hands. Hands that persevered in the face of suffering, hands that anchored me and kept me sane when I was weak, hands that raised three infants into young ladies. These very hands will one day help mothers deliver babies. Another day they will counsel the mentally ill. Hands that will build the imagination of others through her words. If a woman that came to America with nothing but her bare hands can do all of this, what is my excuse? To the best of my ability, I will utilize these two hands, palms up, to teach sixty bright Vietnamese kids every Sunday about the power of love and that in the face of failure, they will have the endurance to keep going Most importantly, I will bring the culture and beauty of Vietnam closer to their hearts, even when it is 6,500 miles away. My mother was a product of war, I am a product of warriors, and my kids will be the products of its teachings. So when people ask my youth kids what Vietnam means to them, they will not need to say anything, but rather show you the beauty of my country through their hands. They will be an image Vietnam; they will mirror it and demonstrate it.

Path of the Bodhisattva

By: Vincent Pham

I fought back the tears as hard as I could. I thought to myself, "I am not going to cry. I am not going to cry. I am not going to cry." Well, I ended up crying really hard. It started with tears trickling down my cheeks and then splashing onto the ground, but the welling began to overflow my being and I started outwardly sobbing.

My outburst came during a Buddhist convention called "Địa Tạng Sám". Thầy Hằng Trường held a very emotional and heart-felt ceremony to commemorate the hard work of individuals through a simple hand washing. Hand-washing? Just hand-washing made you pour all of your tears out of your eyes and all the cries from your voice? Truthfully, washing the hands of my mother and other mothers pushed me over the edge. We wash our hands to clean ourselves of dirt and debris. Thầy is paralleling washing the hands of others as cleansing them of the dirt and stains that life has given them. If you think about the work of a mother, how she tolls in the kitchen to make your next breakfast, lunch, and dinner, while still going to work for at least six hours of the day and still coming home to find more work for herself such as keeping the house neat and proper. A mother has a lot on her hands, literally. The mother has to balance out fifty different chores, responsibilities, and burdens. Her hands become dirty from the excess work; the filth is endless. In this ceremony, we take the hands of mothers, fathers, grandparents, and professional workers and wash away their dirt. By cleansing away their dirt, we free a bit of their spirit to uplift so that they will continue to strive forward in their life.

I washed the hands of a mother who came to this convention by herself. She recalled how she had three children, all of whom are grown up, yet none of them came with her because they were all busy. Since the mother's children were not present, my friend and I filled the role of washing her hands for her. She continued to lament how thankful she was that my friend and I were able to do this for her. She still wanted her children to be here with her though. The bitterness brought her over the edge and she soon cried. I was not her child; I was but a simple volunteer consoled her. In my head, I could not believe that she was crying to complete strangers, but I could say the same for myself. Who was I to cry with a stranger I just met too? Then I asked myself, why was I crying? I answered myself, "You're crying because it has been a very long week of working for these people and you are just tired. You are also crying because this woman resembles your mother." My mother and this mother were exact copies. The qualities of being able to take on arduous labor and still be a loving mother were all within the same person. My mother and the one I had just met instilled to me the passion to love to work for others and the compassion to love those around you.

Volunteering, to me, is a passion that helps you exude compassion, while also teaching yourself compassion through selfless work. My own efforts have taught me valuable lessons. I have volunteered in food banks where I was taught to appreciate having a stocked refrigerator every day to feed my family and myself. I have volunteered at running events that hosted a number upwards to forty-thousand; I was taught that managing the intricacies of such a large event takes teamwork, patience, and confidence. When I work with VCSA, I learn about the community of culture through my peers who share the same heritage. When I work with my fellow Buddhists, I learn the spirituality and morality of why we work so hard. I volunteer in the community to better myself as a person, in mind, body, and spirit. When the time comes for me to take my first patient as a nurse, I will have the necessary tools to facilitate a great environment for that patient. A bodhisattva is a being who would have achieved enlightenment, but chose to forsake their highest state for the sake of others who still have to climb the tall ladder to reach it. I am a person who is willing to give up his comfort and security so that others could have it. Volunteering is an important quality that makes up who I am. I will continue to serve to the best of my abilities.

Burning Incense

By: Van Dang

Pizza was a delicacy in our family. We had it once in a blue moon. It was a pleasant break from the usual staple of rice, noodles, and the flavoring of fish sauce. I was truly excited and looked forward to the occasions when we did have it, or any type of greasy, artery-busting American food for that matter. Late one evening, my mom decided that for dinner we would order take out. After being picked up from my grandparents' house, I sat in the backseat as my mom drove a short distance to Little Caesar's Pizza. There was no line waiting for us once we were inside, so the cashier signaled for us to come place our order. I followed closely beside my mom toward the cash register where she placed her purse on the counter. Being pint-sized and still in elementary school, my head barely made it over the counter and was level to the bottom of the purse. My mom decided to order a "stuffed crust" pizza — a derivative of regular pizza except inside the breading was room for globs of melted cheese. What wiggled its way out of my mom's vocal cords was anything but what she intended to order. Looking like a character straight out of a comic-book, the cashier's eyebrows sprang up as a befuddled look swept across his pimply pubescent face. My mom made several more unsuccessful attempts but the cashier was unable to decipher what my mom was trying to say. I decided to put an end to the ordeal by shouting aloud — "She wants a stuffed CRUST pizza!"

It was then, while my mom and I walked out of the pizza parlor that evening that we made a pact — I was going to teach her English, I was going to teach the same woman who had taught me my entire life.

She sat before me. Her posture was upright, her warm eyes were fixated on me, smoldering with a concentration and an intensity that wasn't normally seen. My mom's hands were tough and weathered yet still retained an air of gracefulness. They were folded as they rested comfortably on her lap. It was clear that she was readying herself for what was to unfold. I devoured what was left of my cereal, turned off the chattering of the Saturday morning cartoons on television and made my way into the dining room. My small frame had trouble picking up the dining table chair so I lugged it over and set it down opposite my mom. As I sat, I tried my best to be as equally as composed as she. Not only was this an opportunity for me to showcase what I knew, but also more importantly, it was my chance for me to be the teacher that day, it was a chance for me to help my mom. I basked in the anticipation and excitement that the moments ahead seemed to promise.

I began by saying the word "crust." My voice was stern and authoritative, as if I were trying to imitate a teacher. My mom took a moment to clear her throat and then she made her attempt. The response I received was something that sounded more like "crush" than "crust." I grinned and quickly corrected her pronunciation. Correcting my mom gave me a kind of pleasure that I rarely experienced. Twice I repeated the word, and twice the outcome was alike. Each time, I was quick to correct. I then saw the look on my mom's face. The satisfaction that I got out of correcting her vanished as my mom's eyebrows drooped and the muscles in her forehead scrunched together. Her once cheerful and determined smile had transformed into a something that was tense and full of anger. I was taken back by what I had seen. It was clear that my mom was frustrated, and in her once bright but now dim eyes, I could see her confidence slowly, and painfully diminish. I sensed that her patience was on its last legs but I pleaded with her to continue. It was then that my mom snapped in a sharp and piercing tone, "Mẹ không có một đưa con như vay! Mẹ nội thời là thời!" (I do not have a son like this! No means no!). She stood up and stormed away. I sat there alone, the silence thickening with each passing moment, only to be startled by the slamming of a door. Disoriented by what had just transpired, I began lugging the chairs back into their place.

That night, things began to set in as the numbness brought on by the confusion wore off. I wished that it hadn't. My thoughts opened like floodgates, racing at a furious pace, questions and doubts abound. I thought back at the times I heard my mom tell me, "never give up"— "try your best — "be strong". I then thought about what happened which was more along the lines of "I can't" and "I give up." The more I replayed the actions and words that occurred earlier that day, the more they stung like sharp needles poking and prodding at an already open wound. The remainder of the night felt as if I was riding atop a broken teeter-totter, all the while trying to fight back the tears from rolling down my cheeks.

The day was Tết, the Lunar New Year, the most important day on the Vietnamese calendar. This holiday was the equivalent of Christmas in our family. This year was particularly special because it was the year of the horse, my mom's zodiac year. I stood in front of the mirror putting heaps of gel into my hair and combing it back in a pompadour style that was popular among rebellious Vietnamese youths in high school at the time. After putting on the finishing touches with a few shots of hair spray, I changed into a newly bought dress shirt and a pair of khaki pants that were ironed and creased as sharp as a razor. My dad helped me put on my tie which was red, a color symbolizing luck and prosperity. With that done, my celebratory uniform was complete. I then made my way into the living room where our family's altar stood, and there, I saw my grandfather's picture which hung on the wall. I took a stick of incense, preceded to light it, and with my hands clasped together

I bowed my head out of respect to my ancestors. Stories of my ancestor's sacrifices and hardships played before my mind's eye, as the plume of smoke from the incense swirled around me like a noble dragon guarding it's pearl.

When we arrived at my grandma's house, the aroma of freshly made moon cakes filled every room. Burning incense smelling of sweet pinewood was no less as strong. The house was filled with every relative imaginable: some related by blood — others never seen before, and although they came from all walks of life, they had two things in common — kinship and laughter. My grandmother wore her most regal of traditional áo dài dresses, which was a shade of rich dark umber decorated with sequin, along with a head dress called a khăn đóng. Wrapped snugly around her wrist was a jade bracelet, and a large jade Buddha encrusted in diamonds hung around her neck. I gave thanks and wished my grandma good fortune and health, and then with both hands, I graciously accepted the gold embroidered red envelope called a lì xì. My grandmother smiled jovially, and just as I unsheathed Abraham Lincoln's face from the red envelope, my attention was drawn to the opposite end of the room where the adults were gathered around a large dining table. There, they raised their glasses that were filled to the brim with wine and other spirits. My dad, whose energy was able to liven up any gathering, made a toast. Everyone listened as he dedicated the evening to the family for all that it had gone through in the past year. With a loud thundering applause, the celebration officially began.

My eldest aunt then announced that the traditional string of firecrackers was to be set off, just like it had been done each and every year before. Everyone poured out into the yard. People who did not have a place to stand stood instead on the balcony, some even managed to climb onto the roof. With a lighter that was mainly used to light Craven A cigarettes, my dad ignited the string of firecrackers. Loud, deafening noise soon engulfed the smoke-filled air like sporadic gunshots from a drive-by shooting. My instincts were to duck for cover, but once I opened my eyes, I saw that the sky had turned completely red from exploded firecrackers. It was against the law to set off them off, especially because it was a residential neighborhood, but no one seemed to pay any mind as they were too busy covering their ears with their hands in order to dull the noise. Maybe it was also because an occasion of this magnitude was not to be spoiled by petty laws and prude neighbors — evil spirits were being driven off and our ancestors were being welcomed home to feast.

With the explosion of the last firecracker, all that could be heard was cheer. I then trudged across the yard, whose ground was now blanketed with red debris, and entered the house. I noticed my mom, who was also dressed in an áo dài, sitting down along with my two other boisterous aunts discussing the latest gossip. My mom was showing the effects of time; her hair, which at one time flowed like an obsidian river, was now thin and gray; her once ivory skin no longer had the glowing sheen that it once had; her smile no longer was as free as in years past.

In my eyes however, my mom was still the flower that was in bloom. Under her tough and weathered skin, I still saw beauty and grace; under her forced smiles and stern demeanor, I still saw gentleness. As I cautiously walked towards my mom, wondering what my aunts were going to say to harass me, my mom pulled me aside before I could greet any of them. When her head got close to mine, she whispered in a soft tone, "stuffed crust pizza." A warm feeling came over me and I couldn't help but smile.

I remembered back to the tumultuous English lesson that my mom and I had when I was a little boy. I had found peace through understanding from a discovery I had made while rummaging through a tin box full of old family photos, It was a black and white photograph of my mom standing beside her sisters taken sometime in the 70's in Laos. Laos was a country that our family found refuge in while Vietnam was engulfed in war. From that day forward, I made a promise to myself that I wasn't going to give up so easily on her.

There is little doubt that the spirits of our ancestors celebrated with us that evening. The moon cakes, firecrackers, and burning incense had welcomed them. In doing so, they helped us find an important piece of ourselves, reminding us of who we are. That in itself is reason to celebrate.

My Mother, My Pillar

By: Velvet Nguyen

My mother involuntarily became the eldest child in the family when her 'anh Hai' was killed by a grenade during the war. As such, she assumed a lot of the responsibilities that her older brother had. Unlike other girls, she didn't grow up cooking, cleaning and taking care of the household. She was the breadwinner in the family, a market girl. She brought in what money she could to support a family of 8 by buying and selling produce and fish in the market. She always told me that she never wanted to get married; she enjoyed being a business woman. By the time she was married off, she was 25 and still did not know how to properly cook a pot of rice. In fact, she burned the first pot she cooked (over a wood fire) at the in-laws, and was so terrified that she would get in trouble that she pretended to fall asleep at the pot. Clearly, being a domestic house-wife did not agree with her.

In North America, my parents shared the financial responsibility of raising four children. Both worked tirelessly in laborious jobs to ensure that we had food on the table and clothes on our back. Despite how hard they worked, one of the things I hated about my father was his tendency to drink and physically abuse my mother. We grew up with my father getting drunk on weekends, occasionally he would get so drunk that he would take the burden of poverty and his hardships on my mother. He would blame our scrawniness on her, accuse her of not feeding us well because she didn't know how to cook. He would berate her for the disorderly house that she didn't enjoy cleaning. In his rage, he would raise his fist and hurt her.

My mother had resented her housewife responsibilities and would scream back, which only served to further

escalate the situation. Each episode
terrified my brothers and me. We never feared for our
safety, but that of our mother's. For our own selfish
reason, we were also afraid that my parents were going
to break-up. The day after was always the
same, my father would apologize and my mother would
forgive him. This went on for years until that fateful night
that my mother decided that she had enough. She was
tired of the bruises and the lies she would make up to
cover for my father; but more so, she was fed up of
having to re-buy dishes or furniture he would break
during these episodes. She didn't feel like it was fair to
have to re-buy things she had worked so hard to earn.

If your parents disciplined you the way they disciplined
us, you were probably told to never tell anyone. Telling
the authorities potentially met losing your parents. The
same rule applied to domestic abuse. You simply don't
air your dirty laundry outside of the house.

One night, my parents came home from a friend's party
and predictably my father was drunk. As usual, he
would mutter senseless words targeted to
hurt my mother and make her feel guilty for not being a
typical housewife. Also predictably, my mother shouted
back mean words meant to degrade my father and
threatened to leave. My brothers and I hid in our room,
crying and scared that things would get out of control.
That night, things did get out of control; or perhaps more
accurately became under control. My mother ran to our
neighbour's house to escape my father's abusive
hand. My neighbours called the cops on my father, and
within the hour, the police were at our house and
apprehended him. He spent his first and only night in
prison. It was perhaps the most degrading experience
of his life.

The following weeks were perhaps the worst in my life. I
didn't know how to navigate this period. My father and
mother had not made up, and my father felt utterly

betrayed by my mother and his children. We had testified against him, and he heard our testimonies in court. These testimonies caused an emotional wound in his heart that was perhaps as deep as those that he had caused my mother. He didn't understand why we betrayed him like that. Perhaps he felt entitled to hurt my mother because he worked so hard. During those weeks, I didn't know if our family would ever get back to normal, or if he would ever forgive us.

Despite the abuse, my father was one of my role models. He worked so hard to provide for us, and instilled strong family values and work ethic. He only wanted the best for his children. His downfall was the alcohol, and the hurt it caused. I know now that there is no excuse for abuse, any type of abuse. Those difficult weeks did pass, and my parents mended their relationship. In fact, their relationship got better and from that point on my father never hit my mother again. I think he simply never wanted to see the inside of prison again.

My mother will never know this, but from the moment she stood up to him, she empowered me to stand up for all the things I believe is right in the world. There is no injustice too small that I won't fight. By breaking the cycle of abuse, she proved to me that my future can be in my own hands. I know that she was terrified when she made that call, but she did it, and it has been the best thing that she has done for herself and her children. She is the pillar in our family, even my father knows it.

[Velvet is Canadian. That's why she spells "neighbours" all weird. We love her anyways.]

A Life Worth Living

By: Quyen T. Truong

When I was seven, my mother threatened to kill herself.

We were in my grandma's tiny apartment - squeezed into the stuffy living room, where my father, brother, and I had been living for two weeks. We had just emigrated from Saigon to Hartford. The transition had been difficult for my mother.

Framed by floor-to-ceiling windows, her eyes wild with frustration, my mother was all fire and fury. Voice tinged with deep despair and anger, she poured all her disappointments towards us. Her words lashed furiously at me. I had never experienced anything of this magnitude before, much less from my generous, openhearted mother.

My grandma responded assertively and calmly. My toddler brother looked up at the din, and turned back to playing on the floor. My father, who had probably experienced this many times before, walked away. I stood in front of my mother, transfixed and terrified. The snow floating serenely down behind her seemed to mock us. My life with my mother would never again be the same.

Over the course of my childhood, my mother continued to threaten suicide, often in my presence, always to get attention and a response from my father, and fortunately was never completed. My mother wreaked havoc on my childhood with her mood swings - terrifying me with her screams and accusations, and worrying me when she completely withdrew from our lives. To the outside world, she was a sweet, generous, and beautiful woman who shared fresh egg rolls and participated in cultural fairs. To my father, brother, and me, she was tempestuous and she sometimes disappeared into her room for days. Once, when she was laid off from a job, she lay in bed, shrouded in the dark, completely unresponsive to my timid check-ins. I felt powerless to help her.

Among the turbulence of a life in a new country, with dashed dreams and expectations that were never realized, my mother learned a new language in her 30s, earned a bachelor's degree in her 40s, and completed her nursing degree in her 50s. She also made sure we had hot meals every night, paid all our bills and did our family taxes, and hosted Thanksgiving. She was incredibly tough and strong, and I found her both inspirational and difficult to be around. As a child, I never felt like I truly understood or knew her.

Now, over 20 years later, my mother and I have a better relationship. My mother feels like she can be more open with me as an adult, so we check in with one another. I now have a better understanding of her emotional triggers, and she knows what she needs to feel balanced and well. The stresses that she put upon herself resulted in a difficult period in her life, during which she couldn't talk about the pressures that were mounting and to cope, she would explode or withdraw.

I used to wonder whether my mother would have coped better if she had a culturally competent therapist who could hear her struggles. But that also assumes that she would be able to talk about her issues. In the Vietnamese culture, we didn't talk about stress and how it affected relationships. We didn't discuss triggers and underlying conditions that result in negative situations. Instead, we soothed each other with comfort food, and smoothed over conflicts and frustrations with glitzy videos and beautiful music. My aunts and uncles diverted their triggered feelings into expectations for the children; my family loved to compare notes on which cousins fared well in school. Instead of addressing negativity, we would move onto the newest piano piece that the children learned. My mother was often absent at these moments, and instead of asking why she might be absent from a place of concern or inquiring what stressors caused her to feel like she needed to withdraw, my relatives criticized her choice of work or simply accepted her absence.

Growing up, I ruminated endlessly about how to help my mother. As I learned about psychology and psychiatry in college, I wondered whether my mother had a mental illness and sometimes pored over the DSM-IV to understand what diagnoses might best fit her. Now I recognize that no amount of diagnoses would've changed the circumstances that triggered her. No amount of medication or therapy would've decreased the amount of racism, sexism, and ageism that she faced in the American job market as a Vietnamese refugee in her 40s. She struggled alone searching for employment, without understanding what she needed or how to articulate when to ask for what kind of help. And while there was work that she could have done internally to mitigate the stress, she did the best that she could under the circumstances.

[Quyen Truong is an artist-educator based in Hartford, CT. Her past exhibitions include solo shows at Providence College's Hunt-Cavanagh Gallery, the Arlington Center for the Arts, the Cambridge Multicultural Center, and the Bell Gallery at Brown University. As a teaching artist and a youth mentor, Quyen is particularly interested in the ways in which art can create spaces for meaningful discourse. The paintings she created to elucidate her father's seven years of imprisonment in Vietnamese Re-Education Camps have been integrated into the Choices Program at Brown University as part of a national curricula to teach students about unintended consequences of war. Contact Quyen to commission a painting or illustration,

or to purchase an original artwork. Fine art is available for sale on her website, www.quyentruong.com.

She's also the artist responsible for our awesome glyph of the boy on the water buffalo.]

Chapter 6: Girl Power

[Christine Ha, MasterChef Season 3 Winner]

This chapter covers the strong women in the Vietnamese community. Inspired by their mothers, driven by their unique challenges, and raised often in a strict traditional household, Vietnamese women continue to overcome hardship and inspire.

Girl

By: Christine Ha

This is how you bow to elders.
This is what you do when you get red envelope
money.
This is the percentage you must save.
This is what you can buy with the rest.
Don't speak unless you're spoken to.
Don't prance around.
Don't sit with your legs like that.
Don't yell, don't run, don't slouch:
That's what boys do, and God didn't make you a
boy.
This is how you memorize the multiplication
table.
This is what you do to get into the GT program.
This is the number of B's you're allowed.
This is what you can watch on TV.
But only after you finish your homework.
Cover the rice with enough water but not too
much.
Always set out fruit after every meal.
Brew a pot of jasmine tea even if your guests say
no thank you.
Let the pho simmer overnight but don't overcook
it.
But what if I don't like eating that stuff?
You have to know how to cook traditional comfort
food.
This is how you take the blame even if you didn't
spill the stew.
This is what you do when your father says you're
no good for nothing.
This is the charred meat you eat, the broken
chair you use, the last place you take.
This is what you can do instead of saying "I love
you".
Don't use English slang.

Don't use English when you're at home.
Don't date until you're done with school.
Don't let a boy kiss you even if you date before
you're done with school.
Don't smoke, drink, curse, or fornicate:
That's what boys do, and God didn't make you a
boy.
This is how you greet your husband when he
comes home.
This is what you do when he complains about
your cooking.
This is the pattern you knit for his sweater.
This is how you can ignore his lust.
Drink these herbs so you can bare a son.
Name your son after his grandfather.
But what if I bear a daughter?
Keep trying if your eggs produce a girl,
But be sure to teach that girl everything she
needs to know to be a
Better woman than you can ever be.

---

*This poem was written in response to Jamaica
Kincaid's poem of the same title, and was first published
in The ScissorTale Review (Winter 2011) for which it
received the Editor's Prize.*

*[Christine Ha is the first ever blind contestant and
season 3 winner of the competitive amateur cooking
show, "MasterChef" USA, on FOX with Gordon Ramsay,
Graham Elliot, and Joe Bastianich. She defeated over
30,000 home cooks across America to secure the
coveted MasterChef title, a $250,000 cash prize, and a
cookbook deal. Her blog can be found at
http://www.theblindcook.com.]*

XOXO

By: Thuy Tran

"Công Cha như núi Thái Sơn,
Nghĩa Mẹ như nước trong nguồn chảy ra,
Một lòng thờ mẹ kính cha
Cho tròn chữ hiếu mới là đạo con."

On every birthday, Christmas, Thanksgiving,
Easter,
and any Christian holiday that my Buddhist
family adopted,
my mother would make me recite this
Vietnamese proverb
in place of a gift.
I gladly oblige because I ain't trying to spend
more money.
My apathetic tongue would trip over the tones,
the meaning of each word disintegrating in the
vast space it has to travel
between us.
But I know she needs to pretend like she can feel
my love
so she will accept my words,
no matter how hollow they become
before they reach her.

Because we left home so far behind us,
As soon as I could talk,
they bequeathed me this proverbial map to guide
me back,
to remind me that I am a daughter of Vietnam,
with familial values rooted so deep,
disobey,
and you deracinate your family tree,
limb by limb.

I gulped in wisps of filial piety without inhaling
and instead exhaled obstinacy.
They never ceased to tell me I was no good,
pointing their fingers at the shallow dip
above my upper lip.
"Your sister's is deeper," they say, "filled with
more piety
bestowed upon her by a Buddhist deity."

My young self yearned for an Americanized
affection
as if it would embrace all of me
but it demanded I give up my Vietnamese self.
I spoke my mind and didn't allow my father to be
master
of his house.
Being the eldest, I was my parent's leashed
guinea pig
The further I strayed, the harder they pulled
back.
My father would smack me upside the head so
hard,
the words "friends" and "sleepover" would fly out
of my brain
before I could even think about retrieving it.
As immigrants we had no friends, and no one to
trust
but our own blood.
The one time I criticized their parenting…shit.
I had a hard time lying down that night.
Oftentimes, he would have me fetch our kitchen
broom.
Knowing I was fucked, I took my time, my hands
quivering
against the bamboo handle, soon to be quivering
against my seared ass.

My mother's rage, on the other hand, is quiet and
builds

until one night she kicks it into my belly
with her heels once, twice, until I stopped
counting
and tried to remember how I disrespected her,
wondered if the heavy heels she wears to appear
taller,
really weighed her down and whether the weight
came from her shoes, her conscience,
or the desperation to kick the Vietnamese into
me.
Perhaps all of the above.

"He hits you because he loves you,"
a phrase my mother would often use
to dry my unwanted tears.
I grew up believing love and comfort came
packaged
with the handle of a broom, the claws of a
backscratcher,
the hard hands of my father.

The day I knew this didn't feel right,
was the day I realized you don't just inherit
genes and money,
you inherit the habits of those who come before
you.
My parents' legacy left bruises on my sister's
flesh.
This time, from my own hands.
I slapped red imprints onto her arms,
the shape of a mutilated heart,
I scratched bloody valentines on her back,
this is how I will love you XOXO.

I laugh about it now and joke that it built
character.
But there's only so much humor can mask,
because trauma isn't a hammer that hits you
over the head

and leaves a bump that fades with time.
Trauma causes a rewiring of your brain,
That sends shock waves through your veins,
the severity of the surge will manifest itself
through the years it takes you to learn how to
love your sister
without the bruises,
to hold another person,
to place trust in a partner,
to openly laugh and cry and empathize.
Because we left home so far behind us,
you survived and preserved
the only way you knew how.
You held me in your arms
the only way you knew how,
the way that you've been taught.

But I'm still trying to find
what we've lost
in the process.

Becoming an American

By: Monique Truong

Immigrants are optimists at heart. War refugees — the subset to which I belong — are even more so. We believe that we can change our circumstances and change them for the better. I'm a writer, so allow me to tell you a story: In 1995, I'm twenty-seven years old, a newly minted attorney with degrees from Yale and Columbia, and I'm standing in the library of a Manhattan law firm with a breathtaking wraparound view, which includes Ellis Island and the Statue of Liberty. Tears are rolling down my face because being a litigator was already pure misery for me.

"My parents did not risk our lives to leave Vietnam so that I could cry in air conditioning in the U.S.," was my exact thought. Epiphanies come in many forms, and that was mine. Liberty and I had a heart-to-heart that day, and I began to systematically unravel the financial stability of my new profession and trade it in for a creative life. I've written two novels, The Book of Salt (Houghton Mifflin 2003) and Bitter in the Mouth (Random House 2010). They have gone into the world and won many awards and have been read by enough people so that I'm now described as a "bestselling author." More importantly, they have allowed me a voice within an American literary tradition that is so vibrant because it welcomes the new.

Most importantly, my parents understood my decision. I, like them, became a naturalized U.S. citizen in 1980 in Dayton, Ohio, but I contend that I became an American when I looked around me and saw here the promise of more.

[The above was first published in The Huffington Post as part of an article entitled, "Great Immigrants, Great Stories: Three Tales of Becoming an American," written on behalf of the Carnegie Corporation of New York.

Monique Truong is a writer based in Brooklyn, New York. Her works include the critically acclaimed The Book of Salt and Bitter in the Mouth. She is also the author of the "A Complicated Man" entry in this anthology.]

As a woman

By: Nguyễn Hồng Vân

My mother is smart. She proudly recalls being the best student in her class throughout her schooling, and even now she enjoys learning new things and is a pretty quick learner. She is hard-working. For over 30 years, ever since she stopped going to school, she has been working seven days a week, usually from 7am to 5pm, with no vacations (except for the one week of Tet, when she is even busier with all the cooking and cleaning), no sick leave, and no complaints. She is very committed. She holds a strong conviction that whatever someone else can do, she can do too. This belief was applied to bearing a son as well. Until recently, I had no idea how much time, money, and effort my mother invested in making my younger brother possible. She worked on her diet, her exercise, her period, her routine, her inner thoughts, and who knows what. Fortunately, she succeeded.

Yet my mother has no friends of her own besides my father's friends and business partners. After she got married, she lost contact with her childhood friends who also married and departed from their homes. She has no secure pension for her retirement because she has never been employed by anyone but herself. She has no real property under her name. I distinctly remember one day when I was quite young, my mother frustratingly told my father, who somehow really upset her, that everything, the house, the motorbike, the bank account, and even the children bear his name, and nothing is really hers. Now and forever.

My mother is caring. She stayed up all night long in the hospital for a week straight to look after my grandmother, and of course, never complained. She is as good as, if not even better, than my grandmother's own daughters (aka my mother's sisters-in-law). I realized for the first time what love is when my father wanted to eat noodles and my mother got right up from underneath her thick blanket on a cold winter day to cook for him. She cares for us, her children. My older sister, who has been married for over four years now, called my mother in the middle of the night, and few minutes later, my mother was already out on the street going to a hospital because my sister's divorced aunt-in-law got into an accident while her mother-in-law and her husband were not home.

Yet my mother has no commitment, no priorities, and no interests besides those of her family. She never understands why I always insist that she must inform me in advance if she wants me to go somewhere with her because I might be busy doing other things with other people. She has no time for herself and wouldn't even take a day off when she suffers from a terrible cough, because not opening her kiosk for one day means some money is lost. She has no decision making power in my family. When my house was rebuilt in 2001, even the curtains she picked were turned down by my grandfather. She feels helpless, and maybe indeed she is, as her husband gradually sinks further into the pit of alcoholism and her son turns into an aimless young man.

As far as I can remember, my mother always tells my siblings and me to study, because only by studying will we get a stable salary, weekends off, and independence. She dares not take a day off because no one pays her for a sick day. She is often eaten by guilt as she can't visit her own mother as often as she likes because she has no break, and on a Sunday evening, she is no less tired than a Monday evening. And because she was dependent on her in-laws for a trade in her early 20s, she is always burdened by the fact that her income is never separated from that of the family. She often refers to my aunts and uses them as good examples of how studying can lead women to a good path. They can visit my grandmother every Sunday. They can afford vacations and not worry constantly about the weather (my mother sells clothes, and a change in temperature can greatly affect revenue). They can purchase things they like because they have their own money. From what I was told, my three aunts were not as good of students as my mother was, but my paternal grandparents were doing well enough to send them to universities. My maternal grandfather fought for the French (he said it was purely for the high wages they paid) and accordingly was considered politically wrong which made university admission impossible for my mother. And my aunts took for granted all the things that my mother yearns for, but can never achieve herself.

So she transferred her wishes to us. I unconsciously learned to look up to my aunts and uncles, and look down on small traders like my parents. For years, I secretly wished that my friends would see me with my uncles and aunts, those intellectual-looking folks, and not my parents. I associated myself with the image of a good student, even of a bookworm, because it seemed noble to me. My early attempt to earn money through small trading (I bought cakes at a bakery I passed by on the way to school and sell them to my classmates who got up too late to eat breakfast) was severely discouraged by my mother. She imprinted her message on my mind: "Never be someone like me. Study. Get a decent job. Earn good money. Be independent. Make your voice count."

I didn't start examining these assumptions (i.e. earning money as a small business owner is not a good way) until I was already in high school. It was too late to reverse the effect. I knew nothing about my family's business and had lost all desire to know because my mother never let her children help her. I was bad at math and acquired a fear of numbers. I was no longer interested in trading and never wandered anywhere near an Economics class. My mother told stories and read to me when I started learning to read. I seemed good at language, but by then it was more of a sense of duty towards learning and earning good marks than an actual interest. My identity was attached to being a good student. My mother was pleased at the fruits of her labour.

I ventured further on the path of learning while detaching myself from my parents' working class, this time actively from my own efforts. I felt closer to things my mother no longer understood, such as computers and the Internet. I mapped out ways to raise my own kids someday that resembled nothing of the way my mother had raised me. I started wondering why, why a kid born out of a working class like me had such a great desire to grow out of her parents' class? Where does my aspiration come from, and where will it lead me to? Until one day my brother told me he might want to take up the family business and I realized such a thought has never occurred to me. Why? Because as my mother's daughter, I have always held dear to my heart the idea that being a woman managing a small business would never bring me a secure, independent, and fulfilling life.

Or to be more exact, a woman with no formal, paid job would have no power within her husband's family and thus no life outside of it. Her life-long, greatest project is me. My older sister and younger brother are not interested in becoming intellectuals as much as I am. I absorbed my mother's message and I live her legacy. If one day someone asks me why I am passionate about women and the empowerment of women, perhaps I will not tell them this long story, but I will know the answer in my heart: my mother embodies everything I want to be and avoid as a woman.

[Van is currently a Masters student in Sociology at Western University in Canada. She spent most of her

life in Vietnam, except for the few years studying in Canada. Check out http://www.kechuyen.org where she writes stories about vulnerable populations like street vendors and ethnic minorities.]

Hai-Polar

By: Rebecca Le

"Oh, hai-polar?"

I nod, confirming my diagnosis, as the woman in the waiting room explains how her daughter has "hai-polar" too.

"Hai" is the Vietnamese word for the number two. We were sitting in the waiting room of the MHMRA waiting to see the psychiatrist when I struck a conversation with her. She wasn't the first Asian patient I've seen here. In fact, I've started noticing a lot more Asian patients come in and out of this clinic.

Bipolar disorder is more common than most people are aware of. What's even more surprising is that a number of Asians suffer from bipolar too.

The Vietnamese are a particularly proud race. Growing up, my parents spent most of their conversations with other Vietnamese parents bragging about their children.

My daughter won the school spelling bee. Or, my son placed first at the state chess tournament. Or, my daughter was the best performer at the piano recital. Or, my son is valedictorian!

No parent ever brags about having a son or daughter with bipolar disorder. No one ever brags about having any abnormal mental condition.

I was diagnosed with bipolar type 1 disorder in 2006, shortly after graduating from high school as salutatorian. No one ever suspected there was something abnormal about my brain. My father even denied my illness upon first hearing my diagnosis. How could someone so smart, talented, and accomplished be diagnosed with such a crippling mental disorder?

But contrary to what my father believed, I have always been bipolar.

Ever since I was a child, I had many nights where I struggled to fall asleep. I remember having to get up to spin around and around until I could not help but fall onto my bed, too dizzy to stand any longer. There were times where I would just lie in bed thinking. I'd make up songs in my head, or I'd have long periods where my imagination would run wild. It was as if I was dreaming, but instead of being asleep, I was wide awake. Once my thoughts started racing, it was very hard to make them stop.

Yet day after day, my parents forced to wake, forced me to go to school, forced me to achieve more.

It wasn't until I graduated high school that I experienced a strong and unsettling episode. The average age to be diagnosed with bipolar disorder is 18. My theory is because so many things happen once you turn 18. You graduate high school at 18, become legal and liable for any crimes as an adult, become old enough to leave your parent's house… you become free in so many ways.

My mind was not prepared for this freedom. Instead of feeling excited for freedom, I became scared—paranoid even. I started to panic. There was absolutely no reason for me to be paranoid. Yet, the fear was there and I couldn't control it. I became restless; I didn't sleep for weeks. My mind was hysterical and my thoughts raced faster than ever before.

Eventually, I was involuntarily admitted into a mental hospital the summer of 2006. The experience was frightening to say the least—it scarred me for life.

There were patients in the hospital with very serious mental conditions. Victims of rape, abuse, domestic violence… Those who suffered from depression, borderline personality disorders, schizophrenia… Then there was me: straight A student, salutatorian, over accomplished...

What was I doing in a mental hospital?

Like all of the patients, I was mentally unstable, I was sick.

Long after my release from the mental hospital did my parents realize this illness ran in our family. My mother's brother, my cousin in Australia, my aunt, my mother.

How did we not know about this before?

It's true that we don't brag about our weaknesses. As Vietnamese, we never talked about our shortcomings; instead, we swept them under the mat, never mentioning a thing.

But as we experienced with me, the more you hold up inside, the harder you fall when things explode. My family found this out the hard way.

Now, all I vow is to be open and honest about the illness that is becoming more prevalent in our race. I do this in hopes that one day the world will know what the face of bipolar looks like, and that though this illness cannot be cured, it can be controlled.

I am Vietnamese, and I have bipolar disorder.

[Rebecca Le is the Author of <u>Sweet and Sour: The Life of a Bipolar Asian-American Woman</u>. Her website sis found at www.rebeccale.com. She also kicks my butt regularly in tennis.]

Vietnamese Woman

By: Anh Hsu

I was born in Houston, TX in 1982. My dad had settled into Houston, TX where many Vietnamese families ended up because the weather was similar to their homeland and provided access to the Gulf of Mexico (since many Vietnamese were in the fishing and shrimping business). Shortly after my parents were reunited, my mom became pregnant with her second child – me! It was 1981 and living in Vietnamese communities meant their English remained limited.

Because we did not speak English at home, my English was also limited. I remember my parents taking classes and reading books at home to practice their English while I was placed into ESL (English as a Second Language). In third grade, I was finally removed from ESL since my reading comprehension and vocabulary started to excel. My dad worked in various jobs fixing washing machines and my mom as a seamstress, yet I was able to attend Saturday school, daycare, tutoring, piano classes, karate classes, and tennis lessons. I am not sure when I'll have the strength to ask how they did it in a foreign land, with three kids and little money – it will definitely make me cry.

Fast forward to high school. I am fifteen-years-old, a teenager, and experiencing what it's like to grow up bi-cultural. In my mind, I am American. At home, my parents never hesitate to remind me that I am Vietnamese. What does that mean? It means I am not allowed to have friends who are boys, I am required to come home after school every day to wash the dishes, help prepare dinner, study my ass off, and go to bed early. On weekends I must attend Saturday school, go to church, visit aunts and uncles, and study some more. Friends are unnecessary. Luckily, I was allowed to have two best friends who understood my upbringing, not because they had the same experiences, but because they were my confidantes throughout our entire childhoods. It's funny how people remember things differently, and of course our life experiences also play a role in how we remember our memories. My friends and I remember my tyrannical, hot-tempered mother who often punished me for not living up to the duties of a Vietnamese girl. I also have two brothers who were treated much better than me—so in addition to struggles with gender and race, I also suffered from Middle Child Syndrome. Triple whammy. I remember in elementary school, if mom didn't like something I did she would make me kneel in the corner, cross my arms, and stare at the wall until she felt like my punishment sufficed. Relatives would come over and plead her to let me stand up but that made no difference. I would kneel there until I couldn't cry anymore.

There was the time I was talking on the phone to a boy in 6th grade. My mom interrupted the call, told him to hang up, and then proceeded to smack me across the face with the phone. I went to school with a visible bruise and classmates suggested I call Child Protective Services. Blasphemy – how could they even suggest that?! There was the time she made me take off my pants so the ruler's contact on my butt would be more painful. My butt hurt like hell after that one. Then there was the time when after a really big fight, my dad escorted her away as I listened to her cry. We didn't talk to each other my entire 11th grade and family dinners stopped. I don't remember how we finally got out of the silent spell but I was just thankful. There were a lot of times, some too painful to recall.

Many of my childhood friends are often surprised that I have such a great relationship with my mom today. I believe that all mother-daughter relationships are complex and what they never knew about was everything my mom did for me in silence and without appreciation – anytime she was wrong, she'd cook my favorite dishes, bún riêu or canh chua.

I don't tell as many "colorful" stories of my father because he has always been an amazing, kind, wonderful, and intelligent man. My dad did everything for us. He worked really hard and taught me the value of perseverance, hard work, trust, and respect. I call him regularly so we can chat about which family member has been the most annoying this week. He's been my #1 supporter since I was a little girl and I'll always be his #1 fan.

I'll pause here to tell you briefly about my brothers. Tony was a terrible older brother and Cory was one of my best friends until college. Cory and I are only one year apart in age and we were also strongly bonded by our faction against our older brother. Tony used to get kicked out of the house frequently. My parents would pack his clothes into a black garbage bag and leave it on the patio for him. He was in and out of juvenile jail my entire life. You know how some childhood memories are so sticky and you just wish they could become a blur and disappear altogether? The stickiest one for me happened in junior high. I had $100 in my backpack for a fundraiser. In the middle of the night, Tony snuck into my room and stole it out of my bag not realizing that I had awoken from the movement in my bedroom. I laid there in silence and let tears roll down my face as any admiration I had for him left my body (he was my big brother, after all, so I couldn't help but look up to him).

Those were some of the stories of my home life. School life was different. I was on the Tennis team, Environmental Club, National Honor Society, and Odyssey of the Mind (OM, aka nerd club). My favorite school subjects were Chemistry and Physics. My friend groups changed during high school. I no longer related to the other Asian kids because I didn't want to wear wide-legged jeans, smoke cigarettes, go to the pool hall after school, or draw in my eyebrows. I also didn't relate to the White kids because I wasn't a "prepster" and I certainly wasn't allowed to attend any social activities or house parties. My high school was predominantly White with ~20% made up of other ethnic groups including Asians, Latinos, and Blacks. Missing out on what I thought to be "teenager" experiences and looking at the blonde girls with envy constantly reminded me of my inferiority – not to mention that all the White kids' parents attended their tennis matches while mine accused me of delinquent activities rather than believing that I was competing or practicing every single day. I remember coming back to school late one night after we had a tennis tournament in a school district far away and Coach took us out for dinner. By the time we got back to school, it was late and my parents refused to come pick me up because they thought I was lying. I cried on the sidewalk and waited for a friend to come pick me up. I survived high school by dealing with my self-hatred of not being White in silence, doing my best to separate home/Vietnamese life and school/American life, and focusing all my energy into tennis and OM. I wished I was White.

When it was time to apply to college in 1998/1999, I knew I wanted to stay in Texas. Although home life was hard, my parents had successfully ingrained the Vietnamese daughter's guilt inside of me. I wanted to be close to my family and I also wanted to attend a public university where there would be more diversity in socioeconomic status and race. I wanted to meet lots of different people and hopefully get over my Asian complex. Attending the University of Texas in Austin proved to help [some]. I went from seeking only White friends to meeting amazing Asians who became my best friends, not because they were Asian but because they are amazing people who happened to be Asian.

Finally, it was time to move on from college. I had majored in Chemistry for four years, and then took classes in Sociology to fulfill my senior objective requirements. Wait, I could have been learning about globalization, women's studies, ethnic and racial relations, and deviance and social pathology this whole time?! I felt ripped off. So I wanted to learn more, plus I wasn't ready to join the working world. I started applying to graduate schools to get an MA in Sociology then consider earning a PhD to become a professor. By this time, I was ready to leave Texas. My American side told me that two years away from home were acceptable. My Vietnamese side would have to handle the guilt in silence. Those plans were foiled. That was the year my older brother went to prison, 2005-2006. I don't remember how long it took before my parents finally told us. They had been dealing with police and lawyers, and there was nothing left to do – he had committed robbery while on probation and would be sentenced to one year in a state penitentiary. My parents wept as they told me and Cory. The very next day, I rescinded all outstanding applications and offers, and applied to the University of Houston. The two years in graduate school were extremely difficult. My parents bought a new, big house so that when my brother got out he would know we had money (which we didn't) and would stop his criminal behavior. At least that was the hope. My dad bought a dry-cleaning business nearby so that Tony would have a job when he got out. Unlike other Vietnamese parents that I knew of, mine never drank or had other vices until then. My mom started drinking a beer every single night until Tony came home.

Life in Houston was rough on me – the commute, studying all the time, being a Teaching Assistant, volunteering, making new friends, dating, working, helping at the dry-cleaners, trying to be there every night for dinner with my parents, and trying to figure out who I was. I remember washing the dishes one night and fighting with my mom. I yelled at her for having no interest in my studies. My whole life she told me that I needed to be successful for myself and not rely on a man, and now all she cared about was finding a Vietnamese doctor for me to marry. In her mind, I was "of age" at that point (age 24).

I didn't care. I had too much angst to settle down. I was fortunate to discover Sunflower Mission and go on my second trip to Vietnam. I raised money through mentors at UH and embarked on another phase in the journey to discovering my self-identity. I loved meeting the locals, visiting family members I barely knew to hear stories about my parents, eating tropical fruits, and practicing my language. I am Vietnamese.

When my older brother finally got out of prison and my younger brother moved back home after graduating college, it was time for me to go. I wrote my parents a long letter about my belief that struggle builds character and although I would hopefully never endure the struggles they had, I needed to struggle… so I moved to New York City!

I finally felt comfortable being both American and Vietnamese, being proud of my heritage, and ready to let my complexes slowly go. Life in NYC was less about being Asian and more about issues with being a woman, haha. It really never ends! These days I wear my heritage as a badge of honor. I am thankful to my parents every day for laughing, surviving, giving us every opportunity to be successful, loving all three of their kids no matter what, and truly showing me that when life gives you lemons, make lemonade. ;)

What have I learned? I am Vietnamese. It makes me embarrassed and proud. It makes me sad and happy. It makes me who I am.

Dear Mom and Dad

By: Linh Tran Q. Do

Kính thưa Bố Mẹ (Dear Mom and Dad),

I hope you'll be proud of me one day. Really and truly proud. You say that to me at dinner, but I know you feel a lot of doubt over the way I'm choosing to live my life. I remember the day I finally got the courage to tell you that I was changing my major from architecture to art. The youngest of five children, I was your last hope. You'd already given up on any of your children being doctors or lawyers or engineers or any occupation typical of the Vietnamese community. The least I could do was be like my third sister and become an architect, someone who uses both science and art. That's what I wanted, too, at the time. I wanted to do what was "right," right being what you think is best. After all, you've had years of experience, more than double mine.

Do you remember when I was four? I sat by your side while you wrote books and paid the bills to draw squiggly dinosaurs and horses. I said, "I want to be an artist!"

You smiled and encouraged me to continue drawing. You wrote books for me to illustrate, but you also wondered how I could channel my creativity into a more stable job.

I discovered I liked drawing maps of fantasy lands— mountain ranges of impossible heights, rivers made of chocolate, and kingdoms ruled by elves. "I want to be a cartographer!" You told me that most of the world had already been discovered.

I started drawing house plans—a house on the edge of the world, my dream house, a castle for one of my fiction stories. "I want to be an architect!" You exhaled in relief and let me draw all the houses I wanted.

As soon as I tried to design a building, I could only think of boxes piled on the ground. The best I could do was to transform those boxes into cylinders. No matter how hard I tried, my buildings never floated from the ground into something more. I told you my misgivings, but you told me to apply for the architecture program at Rice University anyway. And so I did.

Before I started my first semester at Rice, I discovered something that changed my life. My brother lent me his copy of *Flight*, a comic anthology, but these weren't your average Sunday comics. These comics were short stories in visual form. Those dynamic lines, the atmospheric coloring, the incredible storytelling all swept me up into the realm of Illustration. It was a secret place where artists could actually make money and support themselves. A few even had families, complete with children. I burst into your study and showed you this book that shattered all my notions of art in stuffy galleries and museums, but all you did was nod your head and carry on.

I was alone in my epiphany. At least my brother realized that, and he let me appropriate his copy of *Flight* onto my shelf. That was only the beginning. I collected volumes of *Flight*, which became my bible as I poured over each panel to unlock their secrets. I wanted to be good enough to join their ranks. Maybe one day, I could work for Disney or Nickelodeon and find my name in the credits and say, "I made it." If I contributed to the next *Mulan*, wouldn't you be proud then?

College began. I still made boxes for buildings. I told my professor I felt like I was more of a visual artist. She said she used to feel like that, too, but in the end she stayed for the next forty years. I hoped that I would be like her, that all my doubts would disappear.

The second year of architecture was brutal. It tore my confidence and sanity to shreds. Every day after studio, I cried and screamed in my car before driving back to my apartment. I could understand chemistry. I could understand calculus. I could understand Charles Dickens. But architecture felt like a foggy marsh which no map or lighthouse could save me.

I tried to tell you this and all you told me was that my sister, too, cried once about how much she hated architecture. Perhaps if I had a more dramatic personality and threw my chopsticks to the ground and yelled, "I HATE ARCHITECTURE I NEVER EVER WANT TO DO THIS EVER AGAIN", perhaps you would have understood. Alone, I went back to my apartment. My room, my once sun-filled haven, became an ever-shrinking, boxy cage.

I wanted to leave this pain, this suppression of what I loved, and those thoughts of suicide. No, suicide was not the answer. I wanted to be what I always wanted to be. I wanted to leave this cage and take flight. And I did.

You always told me that I could talk to you about anything. The truth is, I can only talk to you about a few things, and switching to art is not one of them. I feared what would happen after your world exploded, that no amount of effort could put it back together. I tried to please you. I lost sleep over words you said to me while you were angry. One night, I dreamed that you died, and I was forced to become a doctor to make enough money to save the family from being homeless. I'm glad you are still here with me, but the dream reflected reality: I would never choose anything other than art.

Once you accepted the fact that I was not going to change my mind, you pushed me to paint and show in galleries because that is what you know. I could and have done that, but to achieve the financial stability you always dreamed of, I know of a better way. While few artists and illustrators are hired by a company, graphic designers congregate in firms or serve as in-house resources. Just as I studied *Flight* to teach myself illustration, I took on part-time jobs to study graphic design. Graphic design is everywhere, even in Houston where home is for you and me, and graphic design can do so much more than make things look pretty. Business can live and die by graphic design. Graphic designers can create who you are, transform you, raise you out of monotony. I designed your logo and flyers for you, and yet you doubted me still. At one point, I held three graphic design jobs as an undergraduate student, but as soon as I graduated without a job waiting for me, you threw me into all kinds of schemes to make money when all I needed was time and peace to hunt for a job.

Thưa Bố Mẹ, everything you've done for me, you've done out of love. I know you just want the best for me, but sometimes, the one who knows what's best for me is me. I hope that by doing what I love and care about, I'll transfer that love and care to others, like you, through my work. That one day, I'll find success—a success you can also be proud enough to tell your doctor and engineer friends, "My daughter is a graphic designer. Would you like to have her business card?"

Con thương,

(Love,)

Linh Trân

A lesson learned in time

By: Isabella Nguyen

The night ends rather abruptly. I struggle to get up. I have not slept well for ages.

I try to sleep, but I cannot. I close my eyes, but sleep does not come.

Beads of sweat roll along my face, and a sharp pain penetrates my stomach. A stabbing sensation overwhelms my senses... over and over again. I begin to cry. My eyes glisten with salty tears. My stomach begins to cramp.

I cannot help but remember. I have given up on forgetting. I merely sit and wait for sleep to relieve me of my tremendous pain.

Even after eight years, I have yet to escape the past. I relive the memory every single day of my life. I still feel the weight o his body on top of mine. His hands savagely tries to rip off my clothes.

"NO!" Please!" I scream as I try to push him off me.

I kick. I punch. I scratch. I bite. All in vain. I try everything I can to stop him, but it is in vain. After all, he is a 16-year-ild boy, and I am only a little 8-year-old.

I keep thinking - this is not supposed to happen. Not to me. These things do not happen in real life - only movies. Oh, how naive I was.

I start to gag. Gasping for air, I reach out for something... anything. Hoping to grab on to something I cannot know and cannot possibly understand... a reason for why this is happening to me. Of all people, why me?

He chokes me, hoping that I will stop screaming and squirming, but I do not. I continue to struggle against my attacker. I feel his sweat on my arms and legs. Gosh, how disgusting it is. How disgusting he is. How can he do this to me?

A whirlwind of thoughts churn in my head: he is my cousin's best friend; all of my family trusts him; I have known him since I was born. Why? Why? Why?

In the midst of our struggle, there is a knock on the door. It is my cousin.

I stop squiring, but before I can yell the word "HELP!" he cups his hand over my mouth.

"You tell anyone about this, and I'll kill you and everything you know," he says. "You got it?"

I nod my head yes. He looks so gross. Beads of sweat roll of his body. His eyes are blood shot. His face reveals a heinous look of lust.

No longer is he the "big brother" I knew. He gets off the bed and goes outside.

I sit in the room by myself. I cry. I faint.

For the next six years, I couldn't remember the event even if I wanted to. Psychologists call it repression, a type of defense mechanism.

It was not until I started dating that I remembered what happened. I never told anyone. I couldn't handle being close to a guy. For this reason, my first few relationships were always rocky and always ended abruptly.

Even now, only a handful of people know what happened. I have gotten over what happened, but I do not forget it. No matter how hard I try, it will not go away.

The memory continues to linger in the back of my mind each and every moment of my life. I still wake up from nights about it. I still cry. There's still pain.

I used to be afraid that people would shun me if they found out what happened. I realize those people were not worth talking to in the first place.

I suffered, but I learned. Now I live with it, and realizing that I triumphed over it only makes me stronger.

Remembering that, I get up and walk to the bathroom to wash the tears and sweat off my face. I lay down and close my eyes. It begins again. I feel the weight. This time, I do not scream.

Troubled times build character

By: Isabella Nguyen

Anorexia. Bulimia. Depression. Drugs. Suicide. And inevitably, guys.

So those are some of the problems I have faced throughout high school. I know it is not pretty, but that is my life in its realest, truest perspective. There is no facade. There is just me.

When I first entered high school, I was in the middle of this great depression. My parents were about to give up on life and were constantly arguing and fighting. They were still great parents to my brother and me, but working 14-hour days didn't give them much time to get caught up on our lives. During the summer, in the midst of being their counselor and mediator, I became anorexic.

It started out small. I would eat a little bit for lunch and skip dinner. After a while, I would just drink water. The entire summer, I lived on water. If my parents were home, I would eat about two spoonfuls of dinner and then make up excuses to leave.

Finally, I came to my senses. I walked into the bathroom one day and freaked out. Looking into the mirror, I had no idea who it was because the person in that reflection sure wasn't me. My cheeks were sunken in. I was pale. I was a ghastly sight. I was so sickened at what I had become that I ran into the kitchen and binged. I ate everything in sight. Then I got sick and that was how the bulimia started.

When school started, I traded the two sicknesses off. I would skip lunch for a few days and then binge. Then I wouldn't eat again for the rest of the week. My friends, of course, noticed this, but they just thought I didn't have much of an appetite.

In the middle of this, I started going out with someone. It was all fine and dandy until the break up. I felt like I had lost everything in my life. My parents were separating, and now this. I just couldn't understand why me. In the back of my mind, I knew there were people who had lives worse than me, but at the time it just didn't click. I sank into an even bigger depression. This time, aside from the anorexia and bulimia, along came drugs.

After my break up, I befriended this guy, who was a good person who was mixed up in the wrong crowd. He did drugs like acid, and offered me some. And through all the "Just say no" speakers and D.A.R.E. program, I still found myself contemplating. I didn't just say no the instant it was offered to me. It was harder than most people think. There was this thing staring me in the face, offering me a chance to forget about all my troubles. How do you say no to that?

I thought for a few weeks about trying some. I even read up on all the potential side effects, health risks, even death. The more I found about the consequences, the more I wanted to try acid. At the time, I wanted to die. I wanted to die. That was the one thought that dominated my mind for two years. I wanted to die, and this seemed like the perfect way.

Somehow though, I found a way to say no and to slowly rebuild my life. I met my best friend who say beyond the mask that I wore every day. He knew that I was depressed when all other eyes saw the smile on my face and the twinkling of my eyes.

When I think back, it somehow amazes me that everyone I hung around had no idea how I was feeling. I think that's why my best friend came to mean so much to me. He saw through everything, and for once, saw the real me. I can't ever be grateful enough for having him. If it wasn't for him, I wouldn't be here. I KNOW I wouldn't be alive.

So when you hear about teenagers who are depressed and whatever else, yes they need help, but they aren't stupid. Problems, whatever they may be, are a part of people's lives. The only thing that should matter is the way they deal with it. If I had chosen to go the other way, I would just be another statistic.

The choices I made, define who I am now. I know that I'm ready for whatever lies ahead of me. If I conquered death, I can conquer life.

[Isabella was one of my best friends growing up. She wrote these two pieces in her high school newspaper column. She would go on to attend a top University, graduate at the top her class, and become a successful partner at a law firm. Isabella continues to inspire today as a Director and Advisor to multiple non-profits.]

Don't Break the Cycle
by Vera Tran

> "Ask not what your country can do for you but what you
> can do for your country."

These truthful words were not only uttered by President
John F. Kennedy, they have been repeated time and
time again by my beloved father. As we have the duty to
pay taxes to the government to help it carry out its social
services, we have the duty to contribute our time to
those whom the government cannot help. As we have
the duty to voice our concerns by voting, we have the
duty to aid the indigent, the disabled, and the ill that lack
a voice. As inhabitants of this generous land we call
home – a second home to some of us – we have the
responsibility to help those incapable of helping
themselves because the longevity of our prosperous
nation depends on it. My father always encouraging
says, "Con giúp đỡ được gì cho xã hội thì cứ làm đi
con."

Like a dam impeding the natural flow of a river, our lack
of volunteerism could terminate the cycle that is so
crucial to the well-being of a society. In return for the
services we receive from the community, through
government officials, medical care personnel, and
educators, for example, we should contribute our time
and efforts to those who do not have access to life's
necessities. In other words, professionals in service
industries are capable of benefiting the fraction of the
community who can afford service or simply who is
within their reach; however those are disenfranchised
need assistance. When I translated for Vietnamese
flood victims of the almighty and ruthless Hurricane
Allison, I witnessed the smiling face of a distressed, but
relieved, mother once I told her that she would receive
vouchers to buy school supplies and clothes for her
seven year old soon who would start the new school
year soon. The altruistic Red Cross volunteers who flew

into Houston from various other states embodied the spirit of volunteerism that could not be defined but could be respected and appreciated. Volunteers helped provide for clothes, shoes, mattresses, furniture, building materials, medical care - bare essentials we often take for granted but many unfortunate families lack, whether due to natural disasters or just the challenges of living.

Unfortunately, some aspects of life could not be simply replaced by vouchers. When I made beaded jewelry with a nine year old girl at the Adopt-A-Kid headquarters, I knew that her excitement and happiness blanketed a more profound hurt and loneliness she suffered. I tried to be the mother who was never there for her, the sister she never had, and the father who she has never met. It may be selfish, but I could not imagine living without the love of my parents, who have been the foundation for a life-long project, a skyscraper of accomplishments. Dedicating time to help, to care, and to nourish others is an investment in our future, or any one individual could became the next Physics professor, the CEO of a Fortune 500 company, or even President of the United States.

Volunteerism is priceless because it cannot be replaced, timeless because no amount is enough, and unconditional because it does not discriminate. It is the dedication to something or someone in whom I believe. It is the devotion to a cause for the benefit of humanity. It is the optimism I have for the future. Without spending time to help others, they could be left behind, and the growth of a society, and nation, and the individual community depends upon the advancement of each individual. The cycle must continue as we invest in our future. Ba, con chỉ cố gắng được một ngày một lần thôi.

[Vera Tran was a role-model, an inspiration, and a friend to all who met her. An unfortunate car accident took her away from us, just weeks after her 21ˢᵗ birthday. Vera

154

greeted everyone she met with a smile – a smile that could light up an entire room. She had an immaculate soul and a song in her heart.

Vera was a star. Her future was beautiful and bright. She was on the fast-track to becoming a skilled and caring doctor, having already been accepted into the UH-Baylor Medical program, after graduating as salutatorian of her high school class.

In whatever little time Vera could call her own, Vera fought for the rights and future of others. She relentlessly gave of herself and encouraged her friends and peers to do the same. Vera raised funds for disaster victims, fed the homeless at soup kitchens, and worked to benefit her community.

VASF proudly remembers Vera every year with its annual Vera Tran Memorial Scholarship. For more information, please visit www.vietscholarships.com.]

Danny

By: Christina T. Le

He was two years and twenty-one days younger, but from the moment I began to understand life, I always had a brother: Danny. When we were little, Danny and I were both afraid to sleep alone at night, so we slept with my mom because my dad worked the graveyard shift. Danny always slept in the middle, so I could "protect" him—the monsters would get me first. I always did my best to protect him. We were both afraid to walk down the hallway from our room to the kitchen. When you are eight and six, the hallway seemed so dark, long, and never-ending. As the older sister, I had to be brave, so our solution was I would carry him on my back and make a mad dash to the kitchen. When we would get in trouble with my dad, as the belt came flying at us, I did my best to cover him as we made a run for it.

Like all siblings, as we got older, we fought. We both knew karate, so when we fought, it was real sparring and no holding back punches or kicks. I will always remember the moment we finally stopped fighting. I was in middle school. We had been fighting often. I was going through the moodiness of teenage angst, and he was being the obligatory annoying little brother. We were rolling on the floor throwing punches when my dad yelled at us: "Stop it! Enough! You are brother and sister! You cannot fight each other. If you don't love each other, then who will? What will happen to you two after your mom and I are gone?"

We never fought again. We became closer and more caring towards each other. If you asked our closest friends, they will probably say it is hard to imagine two siblings who were closer than Danny and I. We needed to grow up quickly and to learn to take care of ourselves. Our parents worked 20-hour days, and we rarely saw them. When we did see them, we saw the physical, mental, and emotional exhaustion and toil they endured because they loved us and wanted to give us everything they never had. We understood their sacrifice. We understood why they worked so hard, and so we tried our best to take care of each other and to lessen their worries. Because of our parents' sacrifices, Danny and I became infinitely close and so much a part of each other's lives. We knew that the greatest thank you we could give our parents was to love each other.

Danny was the one person I knew who would always be with me for the rest of my life… the rest of our lives. We had a future. We had plans. I would be the family lawyer. He would be the family doctor. We would complete the picture perfect Vietnamese-American family.

My brother died in a tragic accident when he was 21 years old.

A big part of me died with him. Danny's death has remained an invisible wound inside me and has left a lasting scar.

For months and perhaps years after, I was an empty shell going through the motions to try and convince my parents and friends that I was fine. I was not. I tried to take care of everything at home, so my parents would not have to. I tried to be both the good daughter and good son to compensate for the loss of my brother. I felt like I was carrying the weight of the world. It is scary when you feel like you are doing it alone. I did not know who I could talk to or who I could rely on. I never cried in front of anyone. I never talked to anyone about how I felt. I withdrew. I could not bear to let anyone in. I was reluctant to meet new people because I wondered: How could someone really know me without ever having met my brother? My biggest fear was that as time healed me, it would also take from me the precious memories of my beloved brother. I tried to keep everything and everyone around me the same. I refused to make new memories out of fear that my memories of him would falter.

Six years after my brother died, I found myself comforting a friend who had lost her younger brother. He too was a college student who had passed away unexpectedly. In the days after his death, she asked me, "As someone who has been in my place, I will be okay one day, right? My parents will be okay, right?"

My reassurance surprised me:

Your pain and your heart will heal with time. Not tomorrow, not two months from now, not a year from now, but one day, you will wake up, and you will not feel like your world has fallen apart. Time makes the loss and the pain more bearable. It makes the memories fonder. It makes living in a world without him more tolerable. Although the pain will creep up on you every now and then, most days you will be fine.

During the first few months, my parents and I could not even say his name. We went through our daily routines, but we were numb inside. It took a couple of years for us to get to a place where we could even talk about Danny or recall memories of him without breaking down. We know he is out there looking over us. For the most part, we live fairly normal lives. Out of everyone, I think my mom still harbors the most sadness and pain, but I do not think a mother ever gets over the loss of a child.

It was not until I opened up and allowed others to share the pain and burdens that I could really process the loss and learned how to live after everything in my world had changed. In the days and months after Danny left us, I do not think I could have imagined being where I am now—happily married to a man who has never met my brother and looking forward to the future. So, as someone who has been in your place, I assure you there is a future that you can look forward to. We all heal at our own pace, but it will get better one day.

[Christina is a director of the Vietnamese American Scholarship Foundation (VASF). Danny was a great son, brother and friend. I miss him all the time. VASF honors his memory every year with a scholarship that bears his name. For more information, or to donate, please visit our website at: www.vietscholarships.com.]

Chapter 7: Intimacy

(Author Jake Nguyen and his mother.)

This chapter deals with being Vietnamese and intimacy, specifically with issues related to marriages and sexuality.

Inside the Vietnamese Closet

By: Jake Nguyen

It was during a long flight and visit to Vietnam where two very personally significant moments in my life took place – the one where I embraced the Vietnamese heritage that has defined me as a man and the other where I disclosed to my mother for the very first time that I am a homosexual man.

Apparently, a sixteen-hour flight to Vietnam and eight beers helped me conjure the courage to reveal my sexual orientation to my only living parent, my beloved mother. Little did I know, I was about to embark on a life-changing journey of self-discovery. It was the longest ten days I will ever know. It was April 13, 2013, and I was rushing to cram my whole life into a single thirty-inch suitcase, unaware that our airport shuttle had already arrived. My mother was waiting for me downstairs while I struggled to fit the last pair of swim trunks into my suitcase. Her desperate holler resonated through the two stories of our apartment building, notifying me that she was clearly stressed and desperate to be on time. She was not happy with my lack of punctuality. Immediately, I found myself having a flashback to the days when my father served some unforgettable spankings as punishment for any filial disobedience I gave them. Why was she so frustrated over a few measly minutes? I just could not understand where her frustration was coming from. This trip would be my fifth time returning to Vietnam, but the excitement and hesitation of seeing my loved ones after a few years was so overwhelming that it still felt like my first time. Halfway to the airport, I sat in silence revisiting what happened earlier. I begin to feel disappointed at myself for not understanding my mother, even after living with her for twenty-four years. It suddenly dawned on me that her exasperation stemmed from a level of uncertainty about this trip. Returning to Vietnam had a different meaning for her. For me, it was just another vacation from the mundane routine of everyday life in San Francisco. For my mother, it was returning to the only reality she knew. It was the world she grew up in, a world that taught her everything she knew about what is right and wrong, and a world vastly different from mine. It was then that I realized the dichotomy of our two identities struggling to coexist. And this was only the beginning.

After checking into Eva Airways, we arrived at our gate two hours early. Our arrival was precisely within the advised two-hour timeframe for most international flights. My odd fascination and obsession with commercial airplanes filled me with much thrill being surrounded by one of man's greatest inventions. I marveled at every Boeing 747 and Airbus A320 that taxied by, as I stopped to take pictures. My mind wandered for a good minute fantasizing about how incredible it would be to work in aviation. Just then, I realized I would soon be trapped inside one of these airplanes for more than ten hours. The chronic anxiety caused by my fear of flying proved to be problematic. How was I going to survive a long-haul flight? So I frantically ran around the airport terminal trying to find a duty-free liquor store. It was the only solution to relieve my aviophobia. I was unsure if the alcohol on board international flights was free or not, so I did not want to take any chances. My mother shook her head in disdain as I told her I would be back. She already knew what I was up to without a single explanation. With a stroke of luck, I spotted a tall refrigerator stocked with beers located inside a Mexican restaurant. After grabbing the cheapest eight bottles of beer I could find, I hurried to the cashier in an effort to conceal the embarrassing fact that I had almost cleared the restaurant of all its domestic beers from the refrigerator. As I walked back to the gate lugging the only thing that would keep me calm thirty-five thousand feet above ground, I thought about how I would fit all this into my carry-on without being so obvious. All this work just for a ten-day trip to Asia, was it worth it? I didn't even want to start thinking about how I was going to deal with the returning flight. My mother sat still in disbelief when she saw all the alcohol I had purchased. "Are you really going to drink all of that?" she asked. I replied, "You know how I get when I fly, mother."

As it came time to board the plane, anxiety started to build up inside me regarding the glass beer bottles clanking in my backpack that might raise the suspicion of the airline attendants. My mother and I quickly located our seats and made them cozy in preparation for our long sixteen-hour flight. A few minutes later, I glanced outside the window and saw the gate we had come from earlier. We were lined up along the runway, the engines roaring as we progressively felt the ground shake below us. As we raced towards the end of the runway, it had finally hit me. I was going to be in Vietnam in less than a day, reunited with the ones I call family. It was all too surreal. I did not know what family meant until I returned to Vietnam for the first time back in 2002, and I had not known what a family reunion was like until that trip. My level of anxiety elevated as the plane lost touch with the pavement. I turned to my mother to see if she was as nervous as I was, but she was indifferent about her surroundings. Her firm posture and strained facial appearance seemed as if she was consumed in her own thoughts. The higher and higher we flew, the more I desperately wanted to be back on the ground.

I told myself I would not touch the beer until at least halfway through the flight - it was a crutch I did not want to rely on. Four hours into the flight, turbulence began to disrupt the tranquil atmosphere that had been keeping me calm. By now, dinner was already served and people were settling in for the night. The lights in the cabin dimmed to help passengers transition through time zones. As people around me dozed off, I struggled to slumber away due to the anxiety that was holding me hostage. I covertly reached down to grab the first beer from my backpack, disappointed in myself that I had succumbed to the temptation, but excited to finally mellow out for the rest of the flight. After an hour, I had already guzzled six beers. I began to feel more relaxed than ever. The turbulence no longer was going to take control of me and I felt great. To my surprise, my mother was still awake. She turned to me and asked, "Haven't you had enough?" I snickered back and replied, "For now." I looked around to see who was still awake and there were no more than a handful of souls. Some had the television light still beaming in their face, while others had the personal light shining down on their reading books. Of course at this point, the alcohol made me restless, wishing I was at the bar with my friends from back home. But seeing as how that was impossible to achieve, I settled for the next best thing: a good ole conversation with my mother.

I turned to my mother to see how she was doing. As soon as I was about to speak, my mother surprised me with a question I least expected. She asked, "So, is it true that you only love men?" I was in shock. Where did this come from? Has she been holding this inside for years? Never once would I have thought my mother would be the one to initiate *this* conversation. The traditional and gentle mother I knew had mustered up the courage to confront such an issue. I had no idea what to say, where to start. I was unsure if the right thing to do was to tell her what she wanted to hear in order to protect her, or answer truthfully revealing this other life I had been living. "Yes," I replied. That was the most difficult "yes" I have ever had to say. What was once going to be a dull and uneventful flight now felt like I was confessing my darkest secret on a daytime talk show. To my amazement, my mother shared that she already suspected. She later explained that she had seen me around with the same guy, even at our church mass. I had no idea she would be able to put the pieces together, giving credibility to the old adage that *mothers always know.* She was actually very accepting of my homosexuality which was the complete opposite reaction I was expecting. I was pretty certain she was going to disown me as her son, and completely void herself of any future communication. Instead, she told me she still loved me and explained that she had grown accustomed to the sexual diversity while living in San Francisco. However, she did give some minor rules and conditions to my "gayness". My mother did not want me to bring any man home or to church, she did not want to see any kind of romantic affection in front of her, and that I must keep pretending to like women in front of our family and in public. She then brought up my father. My mother shared that she and my father had questioned my sexuality months before his passing in 2007. It had broken their hearts to see their only son grow up a different man, wondering if I would be able to produce a family as they expected. I felt an immense sense of pain as I heard those words...it was unbearable. Even though my mother was not completely shocked about my sexual orientation, it was like taking a bullet when she requested to not have anything to do with that aspect of my life. A tender heartache came over me...I could feel the tears eager to escape my eyes. I was yearning for my mother's love and acceptance but did not have the words to express myself. I knew it was going to be difficult to come out, but now I was unsure I was ready for it.

Quickly dashing to the restroom of the airplane, I could see the flight attendant giving me a confused look, wondering why my eyes were swelled up with tears. Once inside the lavatory, everything was released. I could no longer hold in the pain of what just happened. Tears flowed faster than I was able to control. I was not only sobbing in grief, but also of relief and joy. For twenty-four years I had been living another life, unknown to my mother and the rest of the world. I always figured I would grow old and die with my mother never knowing who I really was. As I thought back to the minutes before, it suddenly occurred to me that my mother's earlier demands did not matter anymore. None of it did. The bigger picture was that I had finally come out to my mother and she did not expel me from her life. I knew she still loved me. That's what mattered. My mother was not a bad person for her irrational demand; it was simply a normal reaction out of fear and love. In fact, I was empathetic and understood why she said what she said. I believe that when we reveal our sexual orientation to people, they are not the only ones who have some accepting to do. We, the ones who decide to come out, also have to learn that it may take time for others to accept the news. To simply expect immediate acceptance is selfish of us. In order for there to be harmony, both parties must be patient.

Not only did my trip to Vietnam reconnect me with my cultural identity, but it also made me the proud son of a selfless woman. Being a gay Vietnamese man is who I am. Often times I am conflicted between the two identities. As a Vietnamese man, I am given the great privilege to be a part of a nation with a rich cultural history, and bear the responsibility to pass on the deep heritage to my future children due to filial piety. But as a gay man, I am in constant disagreement with all the traditions my parents taught me. How was I to raise children and marry a wife if that is not something I wished to do? Growing up in a traditional Vietnamese household, loving another man seemed immoral - it was a sin that I could not escape. However, the love and acceptance my mother has shown me proves that I did not have to choose one identity. Shortly after our trip together, she began to truly embrace me for the man I have become. She was no longer ignorant about my homosexuality; she wanted to meet the men I was dating and get to know them as well. This went against all she believed in. My mother and I now have conversations about men and my dating life. We laugh and we cry together. I never once imagined that my mother and I could have this kind of relationship. I was very fortunate that my coming out experience with my mother did not end in a complete disaster. Many close friends of mine have struggled to mend a broken relationship with their parents after coming out. Even though the rest of my family has yet to find out, and who knows how they will react, what matters is that I took the first step with my mother. I very much wish my father was still alive to see this remarkable transformation and to witness the man I have become. I am looking forward to revisiting my homeland very soon. It is an experience I want to relive each time I return. It has always been my deepest wish to bring my family together, despite the distance. Family knows no boundaries and I want to help my loved ones in Vietnam succeed. If any of them are reading this now, well I guess now they know of my true identity. It was not something I could ever build the courage to say in person, but it is a life I have always longed to share. Though society may categorize my identity as a double minority, I see it as an advantage. I am truly honored to say that I am my mother's son, I am gay, and I am Vietnamese.

Con Trai Cưng Của Me

My Beloved Son

By: Jesse Cao

Blog Post Title: *After The Storm…I Think*

Blog Post Text: *It's been one month, two weeks, and three days since they found out I was gay. My parents had found a picture of me and my ex kissing while cleaning my room. Things have died down since then. No more screams, no more claims of not being their son, no more tear filled attempts of trying to assure them I was still the same person. In all honesty, my routine is almost back to normal. I go to school. My parents pick me up to go home every other weekend. We go to church together on Sunday. They take me back up to UCLA with enough food to feed a small village. Thing is, we just don't talk anymore. Car rides and family dinners are silent. It's killing me inside and….*

"TIẾN!" Her yell pierced through the music coming out of my earphones. I was half surprised that my mom was calling me, but then again, a yell like that meant she needed me for something. Otherwise she would call me *con*, or son. I saved the blog post and speed walked to the living room. A minute longer could mean an argument.

My mom was on the computer, trying her best to use Facebook. She was typing, one key at a time, poking at the keyboard, then looking for the next letter. Above the computer was a wall filled with academic awards me and my siblings had accumulated over the years. My mom likes to show off and would be so prideful when guest took notice. My parents went to every award ceremony. I remember how my mom would come up to me and call me her con trai cưng, or her beloved son. I haven't heard that in a while.

"Help me put the photos on the Facebook." The word "please" was not in my mom's vocabulary. She pointed out the photos she wanted to upload. The first photo was from our family vacation in Hawaii a couple years ago. You could see the white sand, the clear blue ocean, the arching palm trees, and our family on the side posed in the very corner of the photo. The next photo was of her in a dress, posing in front of a fountain. I've told her she tries too hard to look good in photos. She still does it anyways. There was another photo of us at a wedding, dressed up in our suits and evening gowns. She chose the photo that didn't have the bride and groom.

At this point, I had enough. She was showing off. She was trying to show people that we were this one big happy family. "Mẹ....Are you done?" She snapped back immediately.

"No, No, No. Be Patient! One more, one more." She starting out choosing more photos for another album. One photo was of me in my graduation gown, diploma in hand, forcing out a smile after having taken hundreds of photos before that. Another photo was of me and my parents in my dorm room after moving in. My mom was holding me over my shoulder. You can tell she was holding on tightly. The last photo was a picture of me on my first day of school, dressed in overalls and smiling with missing teeth.

I wonder what my mom's expectations were when she took that photo. Did she expect her son to grow up taller than her? Did she expect her son to graduate at the top of his class? Did she expect her son to grow up, go to UCLA, and move out from her home. Could she have expected her son to be gay?

"I'm sorry."

The words rushed out of my mouth before I could take them back. I shouldn't be apologizing, but that's the only thing I could say. I wasn't what she expected me to be. It isn't my fault, but you can't help but apologize when you disappoint a women who had invested so much in you.

Click…..click.click…click My mom's eyes were still on the computer screen, clicking through the photos I just helped her upload. "Mẹ?" *Click. Click…Click……Click.* Her eyes were hallow, staring blankly into the computer screen. Her focus was someplace else. "Goodnight Mẹ." I walked away and headed to my room to. I didn't hear the sound of the mouse after I turned my back. She heard me.

Once I got to my room, I headed straight to the bed. I took my covers by the corners, interlocking my fingers with the fabric, and put it over my shoulders, one over the other. The covers held me tight. I took out my phone to engage in my nightly ritual of checking Facebook before going to sleep. The photos I had uploaded for my mom were on my Facebook's dashboard. She had captioned the photos. I'm surprised she even knew how. I clicked the photos and read the captions to myself: *My son on his graduation day. My son moving in to UCLA. My son on his first day of school.*

Tenderness

By: VT Nguyen, Co-edited by MM Zia

Queer. Woman. Vietnamese. - As a queer, Vietnamese woman, I often feel lost as someone who exists as an exile within a community of transnational, war exiles.

Like many second generation Vietnamese Americans, I lost much of our people's language after immigrating to the US. It was through my assimilation in the States that words of my mother tongue tumbled less and less often from my mouth while my mother's tongue had to wrap tightly around new phonetics and broken grammar. My childhood was filled with memories of me and my mother learning English together. Repeating funny lines from primetime television shows and opening Vietnamese-to-English dictionaries next to our mismatch bowls of homemade phở was a typical night growing up in our new home.

But even if I was proficient in Vietnamese there is not a word in our language for what I am, queer; not đồng tính, not "bê đê", but queer. The complexity and power behind my queer identity is too much, yet my ancestral roots are not enough for me to belong as an "authentic, Vietnamese woman."

In my queerness and my role as a daughter, I feel immensely responsible for my family's happiness. Though I have organized in queer, Asian American, and queer and Asian American conferences and organizations, I am not out to my family. For me, as a child of Vietnamese refugee-immigrant parents, our people's narratives of trauma and displacement pulse through my household. And not disclosing my queer identity to my family and loved ones is a means of survival - where sharing one of my identities might result in disownment or other forms of violence.

And during the times that I am hopeful and yearn to share this intimate part of myself to one of the most important people, if not the most important person in my life, my mother, I end up choosing not to. It is whenever I enter her room hoping to start this conversation with her that, while she sits comfortably in her bed, resting her tired, hair-dye stained hands, my mind wonders what kinds of worries and heartaches that have already stained her pillowcases. I instead wish her goodnight and refrain from breaking her heart.

I am then left to think about what it means to build a queer-inclusive community of sisters, brothers, and gender-nonconforming Vietnamese/Asian American and queer family outside of my immediate household. Where, as a person of color, the issues within our communities need healing; and for me, my Vietnamese identity as well as my queer identity needs to be nurtured. Because my Vietnamese and queer identities are interdependent and cannot be divorced from the narratives of trauma, resiliency, and love of our ancestors.

And I firmly believe that my ancestors have looked out for me and continuously do so. Friends and lovers have entered my life, who even as people with such limited access to intimacy, have endured tremendous and at times prolonged violence, loved me in all of my queer, Vietnamese tenderness.

My queer, Vietnamese tenderness is in the way I embrace other queer people and rest my head on their shoulders hoping to alleviate the burdens they carry on them. It's in the way I prioritize intra-community dialogue and education as just as important practices in advocating for our justice, equity, and humanity to those who think otherwise.

It's in the way I massage my mother's beautician hands after her long day at work hoping that one day she can firmly hold mine when she gives me and my future lover, queer or not, her blessings. It's in the way I make it a common and consistent practice of saying thank you to my parents, family, and friends for their support and investment in my growth. It's in the way I look at myself with the unapologetic belief that I am worthy of my communities, our people, and love.

This queer, Vietnamese tenderness is one of the numerous things I give to the compassionate discipline that is our interdependent Vietnamese movements.

To which I say this to folks in the movement:

To my straight, cisgender Vietnamese and Asian American brothers and sisters, I urge you to have discussions with other straight, cisgender Vietnamese people on what your roles are in your allyship beyond just issues of gay marriage, beyond the goals of just inclusivity (and sometimes tokenization), and beyond the intentions of just scoring "activist points" in your pursuits of action and solidarity with our Vietnamese, queer communities.

To my queer, cisgender Vietnamese and Asian American men, I ask of you to reflect on your privilege as men because those prioritized in the LGBT mainstream movement are White, gay men; and though you are not White, you still benefit from male privilege. Because of this, I am doubly invisibilized and marginalized as a Vietnamese person and as a cisgender woman.

To other queer, cisgender Vietnamese and Asian American women like me, I hope that I meet more of you so that we can continue learning and sharing how to unpack and unlearn our internalized sexism, racism, and other -isms from the perspectives of our different queer, cisgender Vietnamese womanhood.

To my queer and trans, gender non-conforming, genderqueer, non-binary Vietnamese and Asian American siblings, thank you. I'll let my actions, both public and private, speak for my solidarity and the feelings of gratitude I have for you all.

To anyone and everyone, our queer identity does not make us any less Vietnamese and vice-versa. We are not obligated to justify why we exist as both. We are and have been capable of holding these worlds together.

For me, the melding of these worlds have the paved way for me to find fulfilling relationships with other queer people of color. These relationships so rich, that I refuse to relinquish my truth and submit myself to this false notion of "turning straight again" in order to live a more feasible life according to how others would view and treat me because easy doesn't always mean happiness.

And though I may not be out to my family or be fully out to members of our community, I have embraced tenderness as places of strength in my resilience and survival as a queer, Vietnamese woman. When I share my vulnerability - confessing feelings of alienation, grieving the overwhelming obligations of balancing multiple worlds, and hiding integral parts of who I am to loved ones - with others like me I feel the most secure in my queer, Vietnamese-ness. Through these tender experiences, I've learned how to define myself and how to thrive amidst a culture that tells me that my existence is immoral and wrong.

So, then, I can only believe in and strive for a Vietnamese community that celebrates my growth. One that acknowledges and affirms my intersecting truths. One that welcomes everything I am and everything I want to be. Because I am queer. I am a woman. And *I Am Vietnamese*.

A Vietnamese American Wedding Day

By: Tra My Evelyn Huynh

One of the happiest days of my life would have to be my wedding day with my husband, Joseph. Joseph is not Vietnamese. He is a white American with European descent. His family has been in this country for at least a couple of hundred years.

I, on the other hand, identify as a Vietnamese American. My parents came over in 1975 during the first wave of Vietnamese immigrants to the United States.

As soon as Joseph and I decided to plan our wedding, I suggested to him that we should incorporate our cultures into the wedding day. I feel fortunate to grow up in a multi-cultural country and to grow up as a bicultural person - Vietnamese and American. Joseph is from New Orleans (which is a unique city from the rest of the country) and has also lived in 7 different cities. On paper, Joseph is a white American with European descent but he has a diverse background as well. It made sense to incorporate our cultures into our wedding day.

We had the wedding at a Catholic Church located in a working-class neighborhood. The church did not have much money compared to other churches but it had a fabulous spirit due to the immigrants that made up that community. The community was filled with hardworking individuals and families that came together in faith and tried to live the spirit of generosity. That value matched Joseph and me.

With any wedding, there are traditions to follow: respect for elders, the ceremony itself, respect for the guests, etc. We were sticking with that. We also wanted to create new traditions. One of the suggestions to Joseph was that I would not wear a white wedding dress and Joseph would not wear a tuxedo. Joseph reacted with excitement as he dreaded the idea of wearing a tuxedo. Having not grown up with ao dais, Joseph thought it was a cool idea for he and his groomsmen to wear ao dais.

I went with a golden ao dai with a translucent white robe while my bridesmaids wore yellow ao dais. At the time, I did not realize how controversial the idea would be. Many people questioned why I did not want to wear a white wedding dress. There is nothing wrong with a white wedding dress. However, the ao dai is such a unique and beautiful outfit of the Vietnamese people that I truly wanted to incorporate it into our wedding.

Another unique aspect we brought to the wedding was that the songs were sung in Vietnamese and the mass itself was spoken in English. We tried to figure out how to make the mass a bilingual service and it seemed this method was easier to organize. We were cognizant that there would be those of American background that would probably be uncomfortable in a Vietnamese speaking only mass and vice versa.

One of the best aspects of the reception was incorporating a New Orleans Jazz Band. This was not a young band. The average age of this band was probably 65 years old. But they played with the New Orleans spirit and that is what we wanted in the party.

It is a New Orleans tradition for the bride, groom, along with the guests to march or dance over to the reception hall. We did a micro version of that where Joseph and I led the party march around the reception hall. It caught most people by surprise since only a small number of people knew of this plan. To our pleasant surprise, guests that first looked apprehensive at what they were observing eventually joined us in the party march.

Also to our surprise, Joseph and I received numerous compliments on how beautiful we wore the ao dais and as a couple, how we looked great in them. Our guests appreciated the bilingual aspect of the mass. We wanted to be inclusive and judging from the words expressed, it was much appreciated.

What really made our wedding day fabulous was seeing each guest walk out of the reception hall with big smiles on their faces. That made all the time and energy spent on the wedding planning well worth the effort. The wedding day was a blast for Joseph and me, and for our guests, because we incorporated the diversity that makes us --- into the wedding celebration.

Parental Pride

By: Huy T. Pham

My parents needed me.

They didn't say so it so many words. But I knew.

Your sister just got engaged to some Caucasian guy from New York. We're going to meet the parents for dinner in a few days. It would be nice if you could make it, but no big deal if you can't.

Right. Always playing the self-reliant card.

I knew. I cut my spring break short. I changed my flight around and paid the extra fees and flew right home because my parents needed me.

Growing up the child of immigrants, you get used to serving as an ambassador. At first, I didn't really understand. My parents were the most capable people in the world. They could scare off monsters, buy the coolest toys, and turn on cartoons whenever I asked. Why did they need me?

But they did. I remember the memories vividly. At the age of eight, I remember going to the doctor with my mother to translate a conversation about her birth control. I remember filling out my own school registration forms.

I remember my second grade teacher asking for a parent teacher conference. I remember being flustered. So I said my mother was busy. The next time the teacher asked, my mother was busy again. She's always busy, I said. So the teacher sent me home with a written letter to my mother. That I opened, read, and then translated to my mother.

I remember asking my mother's boss for a raise. I've always wondered how that sounded coming from a twelve year old boy. But she got it – and I got some chicken nuggets out of it.

I wasn't always obedient. Sometimes, I got frustrated that my parents needed me. I thought: why can't you do just these things yourselves? I want to go play with my friends. I don't want to follow you around everywhere. I know. I'm a horrible person.

But my parents never stopped loving me. They never stopped making me proud.

When I got to college, my parents decided it was about time they tried to do things themselves.

We lost my father's fishing boats in an accident that left him shocked and overwhelmed by the legal proceedings. But after a while – he decided enough was enough. He needed to work. To this day, I'm not sure how he walked into a sign store and communicated that he could make signs, but he did it. And when he thought the sign store didn't respect him, he just walked out of the store and found a job as a welder that he continues to this day.

My mother? She had spent the majority of her life working for a Vietnamese family friend. But there was no insurance. So she applied to the seamstress division of a major department store. When I was home for Christmas break, we practiced her English including how to introduce herself, how to tell the interviewer why she wanted the job, and how to react to questions she didn't understand. She was scared witless, but she did it.

My parents stepped out on their own and kicked ass. I was very proud.

I wasn't sure about this though. My sister's fiancé comes from a very cultured family. His father is an executive at some pharmaceutical company. Both sons were catholic school educated. As a family, they played golf together whenever they could. They enjoyed fine wines and gourmet meals. This family was used to the finer things in life.

Us? Well, we're Phams. We're a little rough around the edges. But we carry ourselves with a sense of dignity. Because that is how we were taught to roll.

It was cute watching my parents get ready. My mother fretted about what to wear. My father pulled me aside and asked how to order wine. My engaged sister, Hang, told everyone not to be nervous. My other sister, Hien, reminded my parents not to use their chopsticks as serving utensils.

And so we rolled into the Vietnamese restaurant. The Phams and the Spittels. Hang thought my parents would be more comfortable in their element.

As we sat down, my mother freaked out. HUY! You have to sit near the parents. We're not going to be able to hold a conversation with them! So, off I went to change seats.

Then, as we were ordering drinks, the Spittels ordered some beer. My dad freaked. What do we do now?! Do we get wine? What is the right etiquette? Calm down, I replied in Vietnamese. We'll just drink beer too.

Then, the bombshell. We don't really eat seafood they said. My dad nearly blew a gasket. We're a seafood family; fishermen for generations. All the dishes we usually eat are seafood. But he took a deep breath and ordered an amazing feast.

We stared nervously at one another. My mother and father had the largest grins on their faces. I took a deep breath and started the small talk myself because I knew my parents were too nervous to utter a word. I wasn't sure if my parents could do this.

But I was wrong. My parents are rock stars. The Spittels would never direct a question to my parents, for fear they would embarrass them, but they (and I) should've known better. My parents are rock stars.

"So, Huy, I hear your father is a welder." "Yes, I weld", my father would say. "Isn't it hard work?" "Yes, but too old now! Can't change!" my father would say while shaking his head and grinning from ear to ear.

"Huy, your mother works at a department store?" "Yes, yes, very nice clothing," my mom would cautiously utter. As the food would come out, she would look up and say, "Good? No, too salty" and smile her winning smile.

My parents were freaking adorable. The dinner was full of laughter and warm conversation. The Spittels may have been more cultured than us, better English speakers than us, but the Phams are the goddamn most charming people I've ever met.

And no one smiled bigger than I did. My heart was overwhelmed with pride. I've never felt so proud of my parents. Mom, Dad, I was wrong. This time you didn't need me at all. I am so goddamn proud of you for it.

Do it for the kids

By: A. Nguyen

For as long as I could remember, I never saw my parents give a single endearing gesture towards each other. In fact, as I was growing up, I only saw the opposite. I knew very early on in my life that my dad didn't love my mom. I didn't know what love was, but from how the dictionary defined it, I knew my parents didn't have it.

I will never forget the first time I felt robbed of happily married parents and burdened by the illusion of a Vietnamese curse. It was during my class assignment in third grade when we had to write to Santa and I wrote, "All I want is for my parents to stop being angry". As my teacher read it, she asked me if everything was okay at home. I was indifferent; it was all I ever knew. I only knew I didn't want my dad to be angry all the time, but as a child, I never knew that it wasn't normal. I just knew that he was the head of the house, the final say, the as-you-wish, and the just-bow-your-head-and-agree-even-if-you-don't. I didn't know that we could stand up for what is right. I didn't know that we didn't always have to be so submissive. But that was a part of my culture and I felt trapped by it.

As I grew older, I wanted my parents to get a divorce. There were nights where the two of them fought, assuming the three children were deeply asleep. But in reality, the yelling kept us awake, and we would secretly pray our parents would just separate already. Or else we would never understand what an ideal and loving family looked like.

My mom shared with me a story that broke my heart. One cold night, she rolled over to the other end of the bed where my father was and put her arms around him for warmth and he shrugged her off. It hurt me that she couldn't even find warmth on a cold night with my father. After that night, my parents didn't sleep together anymore. He would sleep on the bottom bunk of our bed and my sisters and I rotated sleeping with my mom.

Beyond our high academic standards and our emotionally distant father, the idea of marriage contrasted deeply with our Americanized friends. Fighting for the upper hand persisted as a focal point. Subsequently, the idea of the Vietnamese man has been tainted, as our father became an unfair example of what a Vietnamese husband looks like –stubborn and patriarchal.

Just recently, my dad has finally came to me and admitted that he has realized that he wasn't very active in our lives and has regretted it. His story was just as heart breaking as my mom's cold night story. He explained that he never fully recovered due to his sister's death. His sister, who has raised him throughout his childhood due to his parents' early death, was one of the many boat people who had drowned on their way to America. My dad told us he didn't know how to cope with the pain and just dedicated his life to work rather than being a part of our lives. He was always able to provide for us but never knew our favorite color, favorite book, when our choir concerts were, what we wanted for Christmas, or any of the little details in our lives.

Upon an afternoon at the park, my sisters, dad and I sat around a bench where we shared deep conversations, a rarity among us. My dad admitted how he regretted not being an active role in our lives but shared that he loves us deeply. I always knew it although he never said it. My sister bravely asked him if he loved our mom. This was a hard question for my dad. There was a long pause and I could tell it wasn't something he wanted to answer. He put his head down, hiding his face between his arms. I could feel the intense emotions he was going through. My sisters and I started getting teary eyed as we knew the answer. He shook his head and said, "I'm sorry." He told us that he loved us. It was a hurtful to witness him putting his head down and basically telling us that he didn't love our mother, the woman who raised his three daughters.

As I reflect upon my parents' marriage, I realize there are a lot of similarities between their marriage and other first generation Vietnamese-American parents. The most significant pattern is that they stay together for their children even if they are no longer happy. Many Vietnamese-American parents tend to prioritize family traditions, believing that it is best to stay together as one family rather than a separated family, even if the family is already broken. I noticed that most of my aunts and uncles are in the same situation as my parents; none of them are truly in a loving and happy marriage. All their relationships revolve around the children. Although I find it noble of my parents for staying together for our sake, I honestly believe it was unhealthy and didn't agree with it. I sometimes wish they were able to put their own happiness and needs above our family image.

Through witnessing my parents' marriage, I have learned what I want in my own marriage and more importantly, what I don't want. I learned what I couldn't tolerate in a relationship and I learned how our current generation has become more empowered and less submissive. Although my parents settled in their marriage and sacrificed their happiness, I know that I would never settle for anything less than love. I want my future children to know love through the example of my marriage and never have to settle for anything less like my parents did.

Tainted Blood

By: Huy T. Pham

Last year, I did something unheard of in the Vietnamese Community. I called off my wedding. Sometimes we make mistakes in life. But this story isn't about my failed relationships; it's about my family's reaction.

The entire Vietnamese community was invited. Two receptions were planned. My guest list was over 600 people. Friends and family had booked international flights. When I sent an email out to my guests, I got all kinds of responses.

An old Vietnamese man asked if my email was hacked. A prominent Vietnamese woman gave me a lecture on damaging family reputations. Folks told me to save face, get married anyways, and divorce quietly afterwards. Some old men told me that marriage is just duty. And others told me that they wished they had the courage to do what I did many years ago.

One of my greatest fears was telling my idols, my mother and father. My parents looked me in the eye. "Are you sure?" they asked. "Yea," I responded.

Then they surprised me. "Good. We saw you suffering every day. You are our son. We don't want you to suffer. Don't get us wrong, this is going to be a disaster, and we're going to have to apologize profusely to everyone, but don't worry about it. We will handle it. Together."

Then, my mother sat me down and surprised me with a story. "Once, I was engaged to a man that was much older. Your grandfather had passed away, and we were poor. I handwrote the invitations and hand delivered them to everyone in the village. I woke up one morning and I realized I didn't want to get married to this man. He was not kind. Your grandmother supported my decision. She walked with me door to door to apologize."

I stared at my mother in disbelief. This woman is beyond strong. She did something unheard of in Vietnam, especially during the war-torn 1970s. Then, I laughed. I said, "Oh, so this is your fault. Your blood must be tainted somehow." She didn't laugh.

My parents were wonderful. Their response made me feel so wonderful and accepted. There is no doubt that Vietnamese parents are tough and overbearing, but they truly only want the best for us. They will stand by our side, even when we make mistakes.

I told this story to a friend who proceeded to top mine:

"My Mexican husband and I had eloped but we were too afraid to tell my parents. About two weeks later, he was deployed to Iraq. We HAD to tell our mothers. Of course, they both cried their eyes out. Not because WE ELOPED, but because they saw themselves in us. BOTH of our moms eloped with their husbands many years ago. There were no marriage pictures as they ran away to get married out of love, not out of duty, which was very unheard of in their communities. We had done exactly what our parents did… exactly 30 years later. And that is called karma!"

Chapter 8: Fathers

[Hung T. Pham's father cooking in the backyard because he didn't want the house to smell like fish while his children were sleeping.]

This chapter covers our special relationship with our Vietnamese fathers, who can be stubborn and reluctant to share. This may be a result of all the atrocities they lived through during the war. However, despite their complexity, we love them as deeply and fiercely.

Brick

By: Hung T. Pham

Scorching sun beating loudly on our backs
as my dad and I use our hands to pack
bricks upon bricks upon bricks.
Constant perspiration with no hesitation,
I work in the heat with my papa-a day laborer-
who grew up poor, refugee of the Vietnam War,
immigrating here with no knowledge of the English
language for more,
more than that,
for me.
Sweat droplets, salty with anxiety, trickle down his neck
and I too, wet,
lean in to wipe them while he bends back, urging me to
look away
as he starts to cry in shame.
Suddenly, he cradles my face in his rough hands, gentle
and I see him
tanned with dilated sweat glands.
"Look at me son. Even though I've made it to the United
States,
still I am poor, and I am filthy,
forever guilty,
for not being able to give you the life of comfort and
shade
for which I have always prayed."

When he's on the phone with his clients, I hear him
speak with a giant,
heavy Vietnamese accent with little syntactic control,
but I should never forget
that broken English is what makes me whole.
"Papa," is more than my first word, it is my word,
carrying my kin
a sense of belonging that attaches itself to under my

skin,
wherever I go.
Then, Yale emailed me. No, the American Dream did,
and it had me at "hello."
Papa cried in joy for weeks and said, "Hùng, go have
fun,"
"son, take this bright future and run,"
but no, dad, what about the bricks that are not yet done?

"Hùng," in Vietnamese means "hero," so I put on my
cape and flew
3,000 miles away howling "dad, this is for you,"
and I promised to work hard so that we would no longer
sometimes have to go to bed
without food.
Yale, during Bulldog Days, was magical, wizardly,
but I fell into spiraling misery
alone. Homesick, so homesick.
I consistently deceived my *FroCo, "yes, I'm okay, just
go"
when, in actuality, I woke up and went to bed every day
crying
for the first two weeks.
Oh, wait, I'm sorry
is it weird that I just revealed some vulnerability,
because at Yale we're not supposed to do that now are
we?

"…Let me transfer. Let me transfer, now!"
I roared tearfully at
Dean Amerigo Fabbri
who, likewise, was far from his home, from Italy.
"It's okay not to be okay,
and let me just say,
that it's only been a month
and I encourage you to stay.

Listen, I miss my mom every single day,
who still wants to feed me soup 4,000 miles away."

A light in him made me
less fearful of the darkness in me,
too blind to see
that a sore heart and tired feet
were cured with short trips to see the dean
and be
reminded that we
can't know where we're going unless we know where
we're from.

Be still,
know that Yale invited you in,
though your heart may and will roam,
but love came with you to college
and love still waits for the day you return home.

Papa, on the other hand, can't wait for the summers
when I head
home to help him with the bricks still deep red,
strong, hard, with a rusty smell that, to me, is true.
He still calls me every week, praying that I can pull
through
and I tell him that I will because the bricks here are red,
too.

---

*FroCro is short for Freshman Counselor at Yale
University.*

When Prompted

By: Jennifer Vi Nguyen

I. Write, in 250 words or less, a passage that represents your "writing life."

My father has lived in the United States for 37 years, but he will never be Người Mỹ – quite literally, in Vietnamese, a person of America. The Girl Scouts, rap music, talking back and Italian food, he always told me, were only for Người Mỹ. I quietly ate dinner to the quick scrapes of chopsticks against white enameled porcelain and the mutterings of Simpsons characters – an English-speaking Người Việt born and raised in Texas.

Years later, in my American history classes, I learned about the Người Mỹ on slideshows and in textbooks. In 1969, their names were translated into numbers, picked out of shoeboxes, and shipped to Vietnam. They arrived to mountainous terrain, tropical monsoons, and undefined purpose. If they didn't die young, they returned, wounded and scathed. They wrote The Quiet American, The Things They Carried, law, and policy. They became senators and presidential candidates and Secretaries of States, touting their Medals of Valor and their lessons of Vietnam as career credentials.

My father packed his Southern Vietnamese war fatigues and became an egg picker in Biloxi, a dishwasher in New Orleans, and a machinist in Houston. He made scant American wages and wrote checks of thousands of Vietnamese dollars. He mailed them to Saigon and, in return, he once received a hand-written letter telling him his father was dead – maybe murder, maybe starvation, probably politics. And so he stayed, raised two daughters, drank Budweiser, received an American citizenship from the Người Mỹ, and officially became a Vietnamese man in America.

II. Write a literacy narrative.

As a child, I was taught how to use each section of Houston Post: Spread the classifieds across the table for dinner. Make sure that the napkins are placed over the obituaries, throw your chicken bones on top of the used car advertisements, and envelope and crumple the stray bits of rice, the fatty remains of the caramelized pork, and the droplets of pungent fish sauce within the newspaper folds. Throw the balled paper in the garbage can.

Use the sports section to cuông. Put the Charles Barkley trade, the high school football results, and the Astros' World Series appearance in a metal pot. Burn it for the ancestors, letting the flame rise and dissipate into the humidity. Throw the ashes in the garbage can.

Leave the front page for Mommy and Daddy. Set the Oklahoma City Bombings, the Bosnian War, and Clinton Sex Scandal next to the light blue Vietnamese-English dictionary with the worn spine. Stand nearby so that you can explain what lethal injections, subpoenas, and Executive Powers are. After the pages have been flipped, return the Vietnamese-English dictionary back to Daddy's desk. Throw the front page in the garbage can.

III. Write a piece of creative non-fiction.

I was in desperate need of a story the morning I was to take the last possible SAT. I looked atrocious. The hue of my face looked more sickly pale than usual, its tone akin to the melanin of the Pillsbury Doughboy. I had stayed up the entire night memorizing geometric formulas while simultaneously wondering how I had acquired the mathematical ability of a cardboard box. "This test will determine my future," I thought as our gray Nissan minivan inched closer to the testing facility. "I am about to ruin my life."

My father, noting the anxious expression on my face, offered his usual solution of purchasing fast food to alleviate my worries. He ran through the entire trans fat food chain of McNuggets, Sourdough Jacks, Popeyes Chicken to no avail. Noticing that I was already on the verge of throwing up the entire contents of my body, he switched to another plan. Fumbling with the radio tuner, he quickly changed the Vietnamese news channel to the station that played top-40 garbage. "This is Janet Jackson," he said, proud of himself for being cool. He turned up the volume. Under normal circumstances, the sight of a 55-year-old Vietnamese man blasting Janet Jackson in his minivan would make me forget my problems. This, however, was not a normal day.

Never wanting to leave a problem unsolved or his youngest daughter unhappy, my father turned to his last resort. The neighborhood we were driving through was a conveniently familiar road heading toward downtown. He pointed to an old apartment complex. "I used to live in this area when I was not married yet." I listened attentively as we passed by a run down strip mall. "Over there was a place I used to go to for fun," he continued. There was a brief, hesitant silence. "I used to go sing karaoke and drink lots beer. All the women used to love me. I think they still do," he said as he self-deprecatingly gestured to his body in all its penguin-esque glory. I was so appalled and amused that I did not notice our arrival at the dreaded destination.

Four dignity-stripping hours later, my father and the minivan arrived to rescue me from my misery. This time, my mother tagged along for the ride. As we passed by the karaoke bar of my father's yesteryears, I tapped my mother on the shoulder. "Did you know that dad used to live there when he was single?" I asked, hoping to garner more incriminating information.

Surprised, my mother turned to my father and said, "You never told me that."

IV. Write a "hybrid" text.

During one adolescent summer, my father decided on a road trip as our once-every-five-years vacation out of Texas. We drove our gray Nissan minivan through the visible southern heat waves, which curled against the van and distorted the endless stretch of flat, leathery terrain. My father insisted that we only turn on the air conditioner between noon and six to conserve gas. Every few hundred miles, I would ask if we had arrived or if we could stop for strawberry shortcake ice cream bars. Occasionally, my mother would give me a can of Sprite to stick on my head, shutting me up during the non-air conditioning hours.

Along the way, I had picked up green and purple beads in New Orleans and tied raw chicken thighs onto twine, throwing them into the Alabama coast, reeling in and catching blue-shelled crabs with the aid of a net. In Pensacola, I built a sandcastle using a blue Solo cup as my shovel and bucket. In my neglect to smear watery squirts of sunblock on my nose, rubbed off flakes of burnt skin dotted the carpet of the minivan, accumulating as we furthered east. We stopped in cities seeming arbitrary in theme except for the existence of $89.95-a-night La Quinta, for which we rented to cook packages of ramen and pickled vegetables for dinner and to sleep until the next La Quinta.

Beginning in Beaumont as we traversed the Texas-Louisiana border, my mother would scream, "Ai ya!" – each yelp indicating that I had thrown up in another Piggly Wiggly grocery bag. "Slow down!" she would yell at my father followed by stern instructions dictated to me of tying up the spew-filled plastic bags and hurling them out the window. My mother would turn on the air conditioner for a moment to ventilate. As we entered Mobile city limits, the stench of barf lingered in the minivan, mixing with the hot air and enveloping us in pungent sourness.

By the fourth Piggly Wiggly puke 40 miles north of Pensacola Beach, my father massaged his forehead with his free hand, disrupting my mother's cries with a Vietnamese story.

"I used to get sick like this all the time when I first came here," he began looking into the rearview mirror. I rubbed my stomach, straining to keep the acid down. Leaning against the headrest, I swallowed as much saliva as I could produce and diverted my attention to predicting the end of this story. Something about punishment or perhaps redemption.

"On a farm in Pensacola, our sponsors wanted us to go to church and pick eggs," he said pointing to the land outside our windows. It blurred into a mess of brown hues in my peripheral vision. "Me and my friends just got drunk all the time."

At "drunk" my mother slapped my father's shoulder.

"It was always too hot or too early," he continued. My father pulled two tissues from my mother's plush Pomeranian covered tissue box on the dashboard. In the heat, the Pomeranian shed its fake white hairs. Thin lines of pseudo-fur floated in the vomit-scented air and tickled his nostrils. He blew his nose twice.

"I threw up in the church right in front of the priest," he said. "And once, I threw up in the chicken nest, all over those eggs. The farmer got so mad."

"So, you found God after you puked in the church," I said. I wiped the fusion of puke and heat-induced perspiration off my forehead as I slouched further down the seat. "He beat you with a broom stick and you never threw up again, right?"

"No," he laughed. "He kicked me out. I still got drunk."

He looked over his right shoulder and winked.

"I just threw up in Biloxi, then Baton Rouge and then New Orleans. Just like you."

[Jennifer V. Nguyen is a native Houstonian and shares my love of all things Houston Rockets. She is a Vietnamese American award-winning writer based in the San Francisco Bay Area. Jennifer writes about diasporas, displacement, queer issues, and other light topics. You can read more of her writing at www.jennifervinguyen.com and jenvnguyen.wordpress.com.]

You Catch more Trashmen with Beer

By: Huy T. Pham

There's an old adage: "You catch more flies with honey." It's supposed to mean that you get more accomplished being nice than by raising a fuss. In my house, my eccentric Vietnamese father taught me in his own way... "Son, you catch more trashmen with beer."

At work, one of my co-workers asked why I didn't raise my voice and get angry more often. I realized, it isn't in my personality. My father didn't raise me that way. I truly believe that most people are doing the best job they can. Sometimes we can all get a little lazy or lost, it's true, but usually the best way to put things back on track is with a little attention and love.

One day, when I was in middle school, my father and I cut down this huge tree. We laid out all the branches on the sidewalk for the trashmen to pick up. They didn't. My mother was livid - "It's their job!" She wanted to call and complain. My father said, I have a better solution, I'll just leave a six pack of beer near the curb with the tree.

I thought he was kidding. He left a six pack out on the curb. My sisters and I, so embarrassed at my father's actions, removed the six pack when he left for work.

He came home to the branches still on the curb. He immediately came to me and said, "You took the beer didn't you?" I said yes, you're embarrassing us with this old fashioned Vietnamese thinking. We can't bribe people in America. He laughed. He said, "It's not a bribe, it's just showing some appreciation for the hard work these men do. It makes a difference."

I said, "Whatever. Fine. Leave the beer out, we will see." So he did. And the next day, the branches, and the beer, were gone. Real lessons from my father.

At work these days, I save the beer for more dire circumstances, but I am quick to offer praise and support. After all, you catch more trashmen with beer. Thanks for the lesson dad.

A Complicated Man

By: Monique Truong

MY father never read my first novel, which was dedicated to him. He died in 2002, a year before it was published. The dedication was simple: "For my father, a traveler who has finally come home." He would have liked being called a traveler, because tucked inside this word is the story of his life.

My father was not an old man by first-world standards. But at the Vietnamese-American-owned funeral home his third wife had chosen for him, the prevailing sentiment was that the deceased, age 65, was entitled to red roses on his coffin. If he had died a year earlier, the color red would not have been recommended. Red signifies the luck of having lived a long life. His funeral was held in Houston, where the yellow and red flag of the former South Vietnam flies high above suburban strip malls, a place where the sensibility of the third world can trump the first.

My father was a mixture of both. He was born in Vietnam, sent at an early age to France and England for schooling, and returned home with a Swiss wife and a baby daughter. Upon his arrival to a country that, in his absence, had split itself in half, he had to relearn its language. He could speak Vietnamese, but he could not write it. Not a business letter. Not a love letter.

My father was instead fluent in French and English, the languages that raised him. Along with his flat nose and his hot temper, I as an adult would share with him the frustration of having to reach for Vietnamese words, like an itch at the middle of our backs.

I know little about his life during the first years of his return. I know that his marriage dissolved, that his Swiss wife and baby returned to Europe. I know that he was movie-idol dashing. I know that my mother, breathtaking at the age of 20, fell in love with him, and that he converted from Buddhism to Catholicism to marry her. His wealthy parents were relieved that this time he had chosen a Vietnamese woman, but they frowned at her family of intellectuals and dreamers. Five years later, in 1968, my mother gave birth to me, my father's second daughter. Between contractions, my mother heard the sounds of bombs cratering Saigon.

A photograph shows my father in army fatigues holding me. I am crying, infant arms and legs pushing away from him. My mother tells me that this was the first time I had seen him, that I was afraid of him, of his crew cut, of his uniform.

I think the fear she remembers was hers. She was the one who knew enough to be discomforted by the sight of the movie idol dressed to die. From that awkward introduction on, whenever my father left on an overnight trip or longer, I would get a cold. Always a sniffle, a slight fever, an ache. I take that as proof that I had not feared him but loved him at first sight.

My father was not a soldier for long. He soon returned to civilian life and to his position with a Dutch-owned oil company. He was multinational, multilingual and multitalented. He was a businessman for the future of South Vietnam. Unfortunately, that country did not have a future.

In 1975, a few weeks before the fall of Saigon, my mother and I were airlifted out in an American Army cargo plane. His company had asked him to stay behind to oversee its operation. When he finally left, he went by boat. It was a pitiful journey during which he had little to eat, and someone tried to steal his shoes.

The theme of flight, albeit with a different meaning, accompanied my father's life here. As refugees, we first lived in North Carolina, where the license plates proclaim "First in Flight" in commemoration of the Wright brothers' feat at Kitty Hawk. Four years later in Kettering, Ohio — dubbed the "Birthplace of Aviation," also in honor of the Wright brothers — my father and mother had a baby girl. By 1982, our family had moved on to Houston, home to NASA.

This dream of air travel, which hovered in the background of all the places where my father tried to make a home for us, brought with it visions of heavy bodies soaring, of fair winds and infinite possibilities. All the things my father had lost and tried to regain.

When my father came to the United States, he was 38. He went back to school and got a Bachelor of Science and an M.B.A. because he believed Americans respected their own degrees more than the French and English ones he had already earned. He then went to work for the American counterpart of his former employer. The company hired him without recognizing his seniority or the retirement benefits he had accrued in Vietnam. Technically, the company was two separate entities. Technically, their employee was not the same man.

His co-workers called him Charlie. Not an unusual riff on his name, Charles, but to my ears and surely his, it was also synonymous with the military's name for the enemy. V as in Victor. C as in Charlie.

By the time I was in college, my father had been forced into early retirement. He was too proud to sit still and too financially unsteady to stop bringing home a paycheck, so he took a position in Riyadh, Saudi Arabia. My mother and young sister stayed in Houston.

I met my father's third wife for the first time at his funeral. I had flown in from New York City with my husband. My half-sister flew in from Switzerland with her son, the youngest of my father's three grandchildren. My younger sister was already living in Houston.

We tied white strips of mourning cloth around our foreheads. Then we stood and addressed those in attendance. My half-sister spoke in French. My younger sister spoke in English. I, the one who should have said my goodbyes in Vietnamese, apologized for not being able to do so. I wanted to say in the language of our birth that my father was a lucky man, that he had lived a long life. Instead, I said in English that my father was a complicated man who had lived a complicated life.

I wanted to recount the facts of his life, the names of the places that shaped him, the world events that took their toll on his life. Most of all, I wanted to say that I did not believe red roses were appropriate, that my father was a man with many more years of life ahead of him, time during which my sisters and I would finally have had a chance to get to know him, time during which this man, who had circumnavigated the globe, would have been able to stay awhile and rest.

[A version of this essay titled, "My Father's Vietnam Syndrome" was originally published in The New York Times on June 18, 2006.

Monique Truong is a best-selling author of The Book of Salt. She also wrote the Becoming an American entry in this anthology.]

Pho with my Father

By: Andrew Pham

Summer signifies the break of school and the start of spending late nights with friends in my room playing video games. My house was always a hotspot for hanging out because of my mom's surplus purchase of soymilk. This summer holds more significance to me than just that though. It was the first summer I spent single in the last 5 years. The first summer to have a family member die. The first time my dad and I had a real conversation.

I came home around 10pm after spending a day at the pool and playing video games at my friend's place. I can't remember the exact date, but I'm sure it had to be on the weekend since we only have pho on those days. After settling back down into my room, my dad told me he was going to make some pho and if I wanted some. It was the first time this summer that I would have had pho since I've come back so I said yes. The stove is turned back on, two pots are boiling. One for noodles and beef, one for the broth. He makes his bowl first and sits down at the dinner table as I quickly prepared my bowl. All of the greens were on the dinner table so I made my way over there after making my bowl. Usually I would make my bowl and then hide back in my room to finish it. Missing my parents, I decided to sit down and join him. Discourse was quiet as usual. I think because of interactions like this I've grown accustomed to just listening to the ambiance of a room when eating.

I don't recall how it started, but as we were finishing up my dad and I started talking about his past. He started talking about how he and his brother escaped from Vietnam. If I remember it right my dad wasn't raised in the city so it was very crucial for them to escape. They were the oldest so it was only natural for them to take the epic journey. They had to make it to Malaysia somehow to get to the American embassy. This was their only chance at a future. They both were able to get to the ocean but were caught and thrown in jail for a couple months. After coming out, bà nội told him to try again. She told him that they should keep trying no matter what. So they tried once more and succeeded. They made it to Malaysia and were put in Kansas City. After they made it, the rest of the family followed. During their trip though, his dad died. The ones that were already in America were unable to come back to Vietnam for his funeral. I could see my dad's eyes turn red after he said that. The story ended with everyone coming to America. I knew this story had a significant impact on his life, but I never could've guessed what impact it would have on me.

It's October 11th and the Asian American Association was having another general body meeting. We were talking about our different backgrounds and upbringings in Asian American families. Experiences differed as usual, one having stories of being a proudly gay with his peers but still in the closet with his parents. We were talking about our Asian parents and the way they raised us. I started talking about my dad's experience with escaping the war to come to America in pursuit of a better life. As I started retelling his story, I realized escape wasn't just for him and his family. It would be for the families they would eventually have.

I started telling another story about my dad and one of his customers. My dad is a mechanic so it was natural for them to talk about cars. The man started talking about how his son wants a car but that he (the dad) isn't going to pay for it. If his son wants a car, he's going to have to get it himself just like he did. After the man left my dad told me about how he didn't like the way he treated his son. He never alluded to his own parenting techniques, but he heavily criticized that man's style. My dad said that the point of being a father is to give his children more than he ever had. As I shared those words everything started to come together. My dad has been treating me like that his entire life. I've never worked a day in my life. I've been given three cars after the first two have been in car accidents that I've caused. I said I wanted to leave for college and there was no protest. My dad did all of those things because they were what I wanted. They were things that he never had given to him, but that wasn't the point. He didn't escape from Vietnam for himself, he escaped for his future family. He's been able to provide so much for a family of five with his experiences.

Sharing everything I've learned about my dad in that single summer in a small 10 minute speech, tears started coming out. It was the most shocking experience I've had. I never expected to cry. I started to choke as I talked. I just didn't stop.

[Andrew is originally from Kansas City and is a student at the University of Missouri-Columbia, studying Biochemistry.]

My Aging Father

By: ChrisTin Jon Nguyen

Father's Day. Since I made such a big fuss over Mother's Day... it was only fair that I do the same for pops. I called all the kids home...and I prepared what we normally have at family gatherings, bò chiên bơ.

The relationship between my father and I have been very damaged and tainted over the years. Ironically we are so much alike, that it has driven us further apart. The only difference between us is that I can adapt and accept change. My father is a writer and an artist, and I remember at an early age he wanted me to follow in his footsteps. Where ever he went, he took me with him to expose me to different environments. We were happy.

As I was transitioning into my teenage years, things began to change. I started running with the wrong crowd. At the time, I did not agree with the methods he took to guide me and so the conflicts began. Day after day, that wedge between the two of us grew bigger and bigger....until our father and son duo no longer existed.

Through my poor choices and actions, my father literally gave up on me. He was not shy about expressing it either. I will equate to nothing he says....a waste of space. I resented him. My father and I are so much alike that it split us apart. We are proud, pompous, and hardheaded creatures.

Lùi lại một bước thì mới thấy trời cao đất rộng. If only I understood that proverb back then. I think we both had our fair shares of wrong doings that caused our relationship to fall.... our giant egos blinded us from seeing what was right in front of us.

Over the past years, I have attempted to mend the

relationship with my father. I have no doubt that he has also tried to mend our ties. As I watch my father now, it pains me to see how far we are even if he's in front of me. I think our relationship has been so tarnished, that even if either one of us were to sincerely apologize for the past, we would never be able to accept it. The damage is just too much over the years. It was so easy for us to fire negativity yet it's like moving a mountain for us to say...."I'm sorry."

As my father gets older I want to so badly to be able to sit down with him and just talk and laugh. It seems like it's been forever since we've done that.

I remember during one of his drunken bouts with my mother...my brothers called me home to be there in case something happens. As usual my presence there only made things worst.....but towards the end as he was tired and the alcohol really set in... he said to me that I am the son that makes him the most proud....as hard as I tried, I just couldn't utter any words....if I could, I would have told him that I am what I am today because he made me this way......

.......and for that I should thank him.

Transformations

By: Joshua Nguyen

A Vietnamese town grew on top of my childhood home. Our neighborhood once represented the city's diversity with black, white, Asian and Latino families. Now they have left, and my parents found themselves participants in a monoculture within a city: Little Saigon. The refugees and immigrants who settled here had completely transformed a sleepy corner of Texas. Vietnamese newspapers, restaurants, doctors and attorneys, plumbers, florists, bakers, radio stations, TV programs, malls, cabarets, churches and temples provided a shelter for tens of thousands of people. Curved eaves and a koi pond stretched over the field where my brother and I scrambled for blackberries. Red and mustard striped flags waved their allegiance next to the Lone Star flag. It was surreal - this version of Vietnam - made up in the image of the people who lost their country. I was in Houston for my first visit in years.

Dad and I ordered the same combination at Phở Thái Bình Dương. Our breakfasts were a daily affair for this visit. The pho there was good. My dad liked the broth. I didn't want to tell him that the pho wasn't very authentic. The pho my family liked was a bastardization of the Northern Hanoi dish. Authenticity matters little when the end result was an improvement on the original. Two steaming bowls arrived. I waited until the noodles twirled on his chopsticks, then asked him to continue a conversation leftover from our last meal.

Trying to make sense of my dad's stories was like cupping water in my hands. Parts flowed away for you realized the details were lost. Trying to keep track of dead uncles and famous aunts, I snatched bits and pieces of our family's history for a decade now, jotting down notes,, tugging at knotty parts that seemed too good to be true until the whole structure tumbled into a mess of contradictions. Yet, I keep trying. As I grew into adulthood, so I filled in the outlines of who I am - a husband, a technologist, a creative. As my dad grew into his sunset, his outlines faded to reveal all the identities within. The more I listened, the harder it was to piece together all the layers that made up the man.

My aunts and uncles didn't visit often when I was growing up, and dad wouldn't return phone calls from his siblings. He was the eldest son, but he had rejected that role, preferring his own small family instead. His younger sister married a philanderer outside our Protestant faith. His youngest sister married a Mexican man outside of our heritage. An older sister owed him money. A younger brother was a drunk.

We didn't see our cousins, even though they lived 20 minutes away. Some of my older cousins roamed with Vietnamese gangs. One cousin missed a bullet during crossfire by ducking under his car when I was sixteen. I heard that a drive-by killed another cousin as he stepped out of his mother's house during sophomore year in college.

This was the reason given for our distance - they weren't worthy of our name.

Our family's last name, Nguyễn, is the most common surname in Vietnam, followed closely by my dad's brothers' and sister's last name, Lê. My dad crafted a new identity out of necessity during the Vietnamese War. I once asked him if he felt anything when he relinquished his name. Did it mean anything to give up his father's name? He never gave me an answer.

My dad's relationship with his father was always out of reach from my understanding. My grandfather died when my dad was in his early twenties. While repairing the roof, my grandfather tripped and fell. A stumble. My dad described him in superhero terms. He worked on Vietnam's first steam powered trains shoveling coal. He competed in Vietnam's first bicycle race. He lasted for days without food. His voice was a loudspeaker. My dad wasn't home, in Danang when his father died. He was in Saigon, far from his father's harsh discipline, in the middle of his first transformation. He rushed back, but it was too late. My grandfather's last words were, "Where is my son?"

Actually, my grandfather called for Dad by his first name. They were the last words my grandfather exhaled.

Dad gave up both his first and last name in the early days of the Vietnam War, when he was in his early twenties. His days were a series of adventures between a job at a newspaper and rowdy food stalls. He bounced around the capital's pinball machine social life, helped along by his rugged good looks. He sped underneath Saigon's kapok branches on his silver Vespa. He bought trinkets for long-haired girls in their white áo dài dresses.

A courier handed him draft papers after a meal of sticky rice, xôi, at one of his favorite food stalls in Saigon's Chinatown. The military police shipped him to boot camp where he was trained as a private in the South Vietnamese army. He didn't mention depression, his fears of dying or the wrenching upheaval that shattered his plans for the future. "I was at the bottom," was all he ever said.

New recruits were sent to the front lines, often near the demilitarized zone. Most didn't come back. Or they didn't come back whole. Behind the wire fence, Dad planned his escape. I asked him if he faltered at all in his decision to go AWOL. They shot people who made such decisions. "Better than going where they were going to send me," he replied.

He befriended another recruit, a Chinese-Vietnamese boy that became his friend for life. With money smuggled from his friend's wife, they paid off the driver of an ice truck the day before they were to ship off. For hours they shivered in the freezer until the truck rumbled out of the camp's gates and into the countryside. Half frozen, their dirty green fatigues soaked from cold sweat, they stumbled onto a forest road hours later. They each went their own way, but not before promising to dine together in Saigon. This was transformation number two.

My dad was drafted a second time on his way to another meal. They asked for his papers before he could satiate his hunger for a bowl of noodles. He had been hiding in his uncle's apartment for a month and it was his first time outside. He had left his ID under his pillow. The military police had no proof of his draft status, but they were picking up all the boys of eligible age. They tossed him on a truck handed him another set of fatigues. This time, there was no way out.

At roll call, they asked for his name. To give his real name would be to brand himself as a deserter. Without papers, he could be anyone. The first name to jump from his lips was the last name of the woman who cooked his weekly lunches and the first name of a drinking buddy. With this third transformation, my dad deserted his family name.

Back in Houston with my father, I finished my bowl of phở long before he set down his chopsticks. He chewed deliberately, savoring each bite. He often left the choicest piece of meat, crab claw, or crispy duck skin for last. The final bite should be the best. There were too many stories left to share and not enough time. I wanted more answers. I wanted to know about the fourth, fifth, sixth, seventh and all the other transformations. I wanted to know how he transformed from a soldier, to a husband, to the father I thought I knew. I wanted more bites.

His transformations refracted onto my own. We married at the same age. We started our careers at the same age. We both broke our right arms - his from a bullet, mine from a snowboard. I sped around New York City on my silver moped in my twenties. We both looked at the moon when it was bright at night. We shared the same gait, and the same sense of humor. And despite all of my rebellions, he understood why I chose a new name for myself and why I left home. His stories are my unfinished stories.

Again, My Hero

By: Huy T. Pham

Sometimes we don't know what we're looking for until we find it.

Christmas day, a little past 4am. After a family gathering, two grown men stumble back into the house. My father and me.

My mother tells us that we've had enough and should go to bed. My sisters shout down the stairwell that they agree. We wave them off. My father says, "Leave us alone, I want to talk to my son."

And so the two socially awkward dudes sit down, beers in hand, to talk.

A psychiatrist would have a field day with me. Whatever. This is just how my father and I do things. Blame it on the Vietnamese blood. Vietnamese men have "nhau" for centuries, talking about their feelings over alcohol.

My father is my hero. As a fisherman, he was gone for weeks at a time, doing hard physical labor. Fate dealt him an unfair hand, but he did the best he could with what he had.

When I was young, I claimed I did not have a father because I didn't want anyone to know that my father was "just" a fisherman. I know. I messed up. My father, in response, loved me unconditionally. He gave his life and his health so that I could have a better future.

When I was in high school, and realized my foolishness, I tried to be a son worthy of such sacrifices. I threw myself into my schoolwork. I kept my academic achievements secret so that I could work to supplement the family income. My dad thought I was just some punk kid with wide leg jeans and long bangs.

On my graduation day, for the first time, my father told me he was proud of me. I felt free. I was at peace.

MIT started out rough (I had no work ethic), but it wasn't anything I couldn't handle. When I got tired, when I was fed up – I reminded myself of where I come from. I am the son of Peter Pham – bad grades can't keep me down.

Then, I found out my father was human.

I've never told anyone this story. Not even my best friend or my sisters. The memory was too painful.

When I was in high school, my father borrowed a lot of money to purchase a second fishing boat (named, ironically, the Captain Lucky). He poured his heart and soul into it. He dreamed of making enough money to bring his parents over from Vietnam. It was his American Dream. A wayward oil tanker sank that dream.

I wish I knew what I did now. I wish I knew the dangers of personal loans. I wish I knew how to form limited liability companies. I wish I knew how bankruptcies worked. I wish I knew how to litigate against big oil companies. But I didn't. I didn't know shit.

My parents lost everything. We went bankrupt. And my father, my hero, turned to alcohol. He didn't drink socially – he drank to forget.

In a short span of time, my father demolished two cars beyond recognition in DWI incidents. But, it is the second time that will always remain with me.

Freshman year of college. I was home for Christmas break. My mother and sisters were away in Vietnam. It was just the boys.

I was at a friend's house when I got a call from the police. Pick up your father. He's drunk. He hit a tour bus going to Lake Charles. No one is hurt – but his car is demolished.

I can't describe the pain I felt at that moment. I can't tell you how I felt when I looked at my father. Bloodstained eyes. Slurring his words. Handcuffed. This was my hero? This was my father?

I drove us home. It was the quietest drive of my life. I was disappointed. I was sad. I was angry. I was beyond pissed. Even now, the memory makes me emotional.

That night, I fought with my father. I pushed him. I asked him what the hell was wrong with him. I asked him who the hell he was because my father wouldn't do this shit. I cried. He cried. For hours.

We never spoke of it again. But, the memory never left me. That day, I lost my hero.

Between schoolwork, and my father, I didn't know how to cope. At the time, I didn't know what was bothering me, but I grew depressed. I slept and ate a lot of bad Chinese food. Between Christmas Break and Spring Break, I gained a lot of weight. No joke. I cleared 200 easy.

I lost the weight by the time summer hit, but I never felt the same. That memory has always haunted me. In retrospect, it was what brought me back to Houston after graduation.

I may have learned that my father was human – but I didn't love him any less. It was my turn to take care of him.

My sister and I tried our best. My parents had no credit. So we co-signed their credit cards, their car loans, and moved with them into another house. We paid the bills until they were employed again.

When I finally felt things were getting better, I ran away from responsibility. I went to grad school. All year, I struggled with the idea of leaving Houston. Consciously, I wanted to leave badly – but my heart wouldn't let me. Now I know why – the memory of that night still haunted me.

Christmas Day 2008. 4:00AM. Father and son.

I start off. I never have been so blunt. Dad, I love you. I don't want you to think I don't love you just because I might leave Houston. I will always be here for you.

He laughs. Son, some people might not think you love me if you leave. I don't care. I know you love me. You are my pride. You took care of me. I understand. You need to go. But don't worry about me. Our bankruptcy is almost up. I have a good job. I have things under control.

The words meant a lot. But not as much as the way he said it. He said it confidently. He said it with strength. He said it with dignity. He said it like my father.

Ever since Christmas, I have felt free. Free of obligation, free of concern, and free of painful memories. I didn't know I needed this – but I did.

This is the greatest achievement of my life. Forget grades. Forget degrees. I made my father proud. I restored him to the man he was. He is my hero again.

I walk with a bounce in my step. A big smile on my face. I am at peace.

I found what I didn't know I needed.

I have my hero again.

Another Ten Minutes

By: Matthew Tran

I don't always drive under the speed limit. When I do, the streets are empty and dark; they give way in my headlights. Having just dropped off my father's obnoxiously loud friend, Tam, who enjoys imparting platitudes like a Shel Silverstein poem, I am driving home. Next to me, just as filled with drink as his friend, is my father. He accompanies me every time I have to drop off Tam. Car rides at three in the morning mean there are no distractions—no TV sports, no mother, no little sister, no friends, no cigarettes, no beers. Just father and son. Car rides like these force us to do something we usually never do: talk.

Because I can understand Vietnamese better than I can speak it, our conversation is mostly me listening to my father speak without inhibition. It lasts the distance between Tam's home and ours—about ten minutes (sometimes more if I time myself to arrive at every stoplight just as it's turning red). The brevity makes our chats precious as though they were time capsules to be stored away until the next car ride. In our twelve-year old Toyota Avalon, my father lowers his voice to a somber level and rambles on about his life. In these car rides, my father, usually jocular when drunk, or awkwardly reserved when sober, changes.

My father is a proud man. During a part of my middle school and all of high school, he was unemployed or as he liked to tell me during application cycles, "put me down as self-employed, boy." For a total of six years, he spent his days lounging on our backyard porch. My father built the porch with profits from his grocery, named Quê Hương, Vietnamese for home; shortly thereafter, he lost his store—but he still had his porch. It was impressive. He made it from Philippine Mahogany and finished it with a thick layer of white paint. It had a farmhouse feel to it. Because this was Houston, he even installed nifty mist sprayers. The whole time of his unemployment was spent on that back porch; the smoke and smell from his cigarettes seeped deep into the wood.

During most of the day, I rarely saw my father, who only occasionally came in for another can of cheap beer. I actually saw my mother, who worked all day, almost every day, more often than my father. He would sit out on the porch and make plan after plan—calling unsupportive banks, negotiating leases, hiring unreliable companies—to restart his market. And no matter how many times he failed—because of a lethargic architect, a negligent construction company, or draconian licenses—he never once considered trying to look for a job. He adamantly refused to work for someone else. And for my mother, who worked as a waitress all her life, answering both to her customers and to her boss, this refusal nearly drove her mad. When I turned six, I told my father I wanted to be a movie actor when I grew up. He said I could star in someone else's production, but only if I was a fool. Authority sickened him.

My father reported to no one, except perhaps my mother, who called him Mr. Mom. He was the kind of Mr. Mom who took on the title but not the duties that came with it. Mr. Mom always said he'd tidy the living room— messy with books, newspapers, magazines, dirty plates, clothes, leftovers—but these promises were just sweet nothings to my mother. As a former proprietor of a supermarket, he understood food. He understood enough to cook meals so well that people said he should open up a restaurant. Last year, he did, somewhat.

Giving up on restarting his grocery, my father was convinced he could turn around a failing Vietnamese café that his younger brother abandoned for a better job in Singapore. But according to his 1040 I asked for to file my FAFSA, he hasn't turned a profit. Adding lines 7, "wages, salaries, tips, etc.," and 12, "business income or (loss)," meant adding his negative "profits" from my mother's wages. In one of these car rides, I asked about the café, and, as usual, he just shook his head. "No good. Business is slow."

When my aunts, who worked in the same successful— relative to my father's café—nail shop together, invited him and his family to a fine restaurant, only my sister and I would go. My mother was always working, while my father, during his unemployment, refused to let others pay for his meal. "Just tell them I'm busy with work," he said. Only on car rides with my father, in a drunken daze, his face so red with drink he looked sunburned, does his pride fade enough for him to talk.

"OK, boy. Let me tell you." My father divulged the rise and fall of his business. In his attempt to restart his market or start a new convenient store, his older brother—with ashy-dark skin, with hair only on the rim of his head like Larry Fine, and with a beer belly that stretches XXL—stands in the way. My uncle, as the oldest living brother, wants his siblings to never exceed his success, even if it meant deceiving and betraying. For my father, water of the womb is thin. He told me how my older cousin summarized my older uncle, "Once you owe him a favor, you owe him your life." Underneath my older uncle's generous exterior is a king afraid to lose his throne. Still, they are banned from each other's homes.

These car rides make me realize that when I look back on our lives thus far, my father and I are as different as liquor and liquorice. My father likes to joke that he found me, a doe-eyed kid, in a trashcan.

"Don't you think you have the best baba in the world?" I now think he said that because when he was my age, he understood a hunger so deep and ravenous that it becomes a constant droning companion who clings inside his stomach lining as he crossed the Pacific alone. My father named me Phúc—which means blessed in Vietnamese—for all the blessings he never had. When he still had his grocery, he let homeless men, bearded, bundled-up, with clothes that smelled of animals and rain, beg for money at the entrance. My father was drawn to weakness.

And even though he tolerates none in me, he welcomes it in others. But this is all I've ever done for him—record things, traffic in words. If I am to understand anything— why this divide exists—I have to remain silent, drive slowly, and let him talk as I listen in the darkness.

On this particular night, my father begins to talk about his life. On April 21, 1975, around 7:00 PM, he watched his uncle with Parkinson's lament, tears dropping and unpredictably landing as his head uncontrollably shook. In that moment, Nguyen Van Thieu, president of South Vietnam, resigned on national television, a sign that Saigon would shortly fall to the Viet Cong. The VC had already conquered the other major cities of Hue, Da Nang, and Ban Me Thuot. Another uncle, a police officer from the South, came with an offer for my father and his older brother. My father says, "I was fourteen, and there was one more spot on the boat. It was mine for the taking." As the middle child of fourteen and with three younger brothers and three younger sisters, he declined. A week later, he watched the silent, hopeless disorder of fleeing soldiers, some abandoning their uniforms on the curbs, others lying dead and un-mourned in the mounds of trash. Saigon had fallen. Even though the new Communist government promised not to hurt civilians, the streets – without people hustling to their offices, without people cheerfully calling out hellos to their neighbors, without people riding noisy mopeds – remained deserted.

Seven minutes into his story, I drive by Specs, a Texas liquor and foods store. My father tells me to remind him tomorrow morning that the store would be having a sale the next day. And just like that, he continues with his story.

In the coming days after the fall of Saigon, all of his friends, families, neighbors searched frantically for a strange flag. It was the flag of the Provisional Revolutionary Government, and it began to spring up in front of people's homes like weeds. The flag was split horizontally with color: red on top and light blue on the bottom, while a yellow star marked the center. My grandfather forced my father, wandering from store to store, until the colors from flags already hung outside made him increasingly anxious and dizzy as he looked down any street, to search for the flag. If a home didn't have this flag, then the government suspected the owners of treason. He couldn't bear to come home empty-handed, so he searched until his feet blistered, until his shirt dripped beads of sweat, until the sun disappeared, until he finally found one.

My father's voice trails off as I pull into the driveway. Before he can finish this small glimpse into his past, we arrive at home.

Two weeks later, on a steamy night that reminds my father of Vietnam, Tam comes by again to visit him like a stray dog in the rain. Until I learned to drive, I never knew how accessible my father was; I just had to approach him by the right door. These are the longest windows of time I have with him – a windowpane opens because my father needs someone sober. In the middle of the night, I am right where I want to be: driving Tam home, and then, driving my father home.

For a man of his age, forty-eight, short, graying in his hair and mustache, always wearing the same beige jacket, he seems to be enjoying himself, laughing, as he picks up the thread of the previous story.

My father was eighteen, and he felt invincible. On a deserted beachfront in deep shadow, high docks abandoned after the war, in a dead silence, and a rising sun, my father and several other men bribed their way onto a boat chartered for the Philippines. Two or three miles out to sea, my father heard gunshots that reminded him of his childhood early during the Vietnam War. A bullet pierced the rudder man, and he collapsed.

I hear my father's voice break slightly before he smiles like a happy drunk and begins again.

Peering out from under his tarp, he saw another man try to take over the steering, and then he too was shot. Grinning now to conceal the tension, he describes how three others attempted to take over the role of steering, but all three fell. When it was my father's turn to take the rudder, he said, "Fuck it. I wouldn't be dumb like them." His boat surrendered to the Communists.

Then we are home. I feel once more how simple our relationship has come to be: a car ride, some alcohol, and a road before us. Nothing else.

On yet another chilly night, my father continues his story.

Up from the wood planks of the boat, up from the empty, hot beach and rotting smell of dead fish, my father and his companions marched. The Communist army officers herded them back through a small village towards a reeducation camp. But my father thought he was clever. He feigned a fainting spell. The soldier took pity on him and granted him permission to search for water. When he turned the corner of a straw hut, he bolted. He left behind his uncle, who was whipped in reeducation camp. My father sought refuge in the home of strangers, a widow and her daughter; they hid him under some straw and floorboards as Communist officers knocked on their doors, searching for him. He escaped.

My father said the daughter started to fancy him, but he explained, "I didn't like her at all. I liked your mother better when I met her later."

At this moment, my mother turns on the garage lights to welcome us home. I watch my father stumble into our pink-brick house and go into the kitchen for a snack. With a quick glance, my father says, "Good night, boy."

At that moment, I realize – that in the car – my father has not been speaking to me as one would speak to his only son, but as he would speak to his friend, a stranger, anyone. Each car ride exposes a still of my father's life like a roll of film, and Tam unwittingly delivers each frame.

And this is how my father becomes known to me, ten minutes at a time.

Count the Moments

by Hanh Tran

Count the moments as they pass by.

The time that dad forgot your birthday and the tears that
stained your eyes.

Count the moments on how hard he tries. He writes our
birthdays on the calendar now, and gets frustrated when
we don't return his calls.

He gives his best, tries his best, and hopes for the best,
but if you can only see how hard he tries.

Count the moments those hard feelings that left when
we sang and smiled with 65 candles on his cake.

When he yells and you laugh, he rubs his head, and
can't believe how much you share.

He is proud of his country, he is proud of his roots, and
he'll tell you the way it is with his thick accent.

He came here with nothing, and then there was us. His
hopes and dreams in the American colors.

All he wants is for you to listen. Smile, nod, and lean in.
He'll show you his heart, he'll do his best. He helped to
get you here, he'll do his best with the rest.

Count the moments when you hear his whistle. His
hands in a stance of words of wisdom. He's dressed to
the nines, the proudest pop ever. He beams and smiles
when you come hither. He loves you and adores you til
forever.

Count the moments.

Chapter 9: War Remnants

This chapter covers the war remnants within our identities.

Not all that glitters is gold

By: Kim Nguyen, BKA King Kimbit, SKA Poetic Justice

I know...
But whenever I dream of Viet Nam,
I see the sea that surrounds it and the glistening on its
surface
From what appears to be
Rays of lights' reflection
And here, my logic plays deceptive because the
glittering golden beams I see
Is really GOLD that's being reflected.

Whatever treasures lay at the bottom, I may never get to
discover...
But the gold I see glisten
Is that of the blood and bones of my sisters and
brothers;
Those who were not so much blessed with the same
fortunes met by my mother and father
Whom had gotten up and left in the same haphazard
manner
Fleeing for freedom by leaving their motherland
In attempts to escape the aftermath
Of the war

Which, contrary to ignorant beliefs,
Was not us against the Americans.
Viet Nam was a civil war,
Or more like a military conflict
Between the South and the North.
Fearing the expansion of the northern communists,
America sent soldiers down south
To help us win
...but then the U.S. left and so Saigon fell to Ho Chi
Minh
On the 30th of April
1975

UNITY wasn't quite the right word to describe the cusp
of the divide between the
North and the South because our people were devoured
by the hunger for this power

Leaving the country at that time was considered illegal,
But despite those consequences,
To stay there
Was lethal

So, for countless nights upon nights, it was
Run to the boats before they see you.
Forget everything you were; you are now Vietnamese
Boat People
Take along nothing with you other than the amount of
gold that you can hold in your anatomy
So you can sell it when you land
But don't fret or fear if you end up empty handed

Just appreciate getting past the oceans because that
alone was
Not a fate that a lot of us had the privilege of holding.

The feeble little fishing boats we were armed with often
faced hardships
Whether we were fighting off

Disease
Pirates
Or being blown to bits by harsh winds
Our head spaces hoodwinked by our hunger and
exhaustion;
Though we know blood's thicker than water, there's not
much difference when you're starving...

And making it to land was still not yet victory;
Some places we landed would pack us back into our
boats like sardines and
Push us back out to sea

So

Many times, we had to break our boats upon arrival
Because we could no longer afford to sink and had no
energy left to swim

With an escape plan so shady, we knew our chances of
survival would be slim

Still, we had that
Get free or die trying mentality
So we had to get free
But only half of us succeeded
(Although no specific amount of countless casualties
could be accounted for since no one knows for sure how
many had left)

But you can count on this:

Though we may have lost our land
And half our people,
Tall and strong we shall stand and
Our flags will keep on
Being raised
All over the world

Much like our children.
And it will be through them that our stories
And our spirits
Keep on living

---

*[Kim Nguyen is from Ottawa, Canada and is a spoken
word artist. This piece is even better performed. Please
check out her YouTube Channel, under KingKimbit for
the live performance]*

The Stitch

By: Tam Lontok

One month after the wedding, I came home to a UPS box placed on my dresser and it was addressed from Ms. Peg Olson. Upon reading her name, I immediately opened the box with my husband beside me.

A tear shed after reading the first paragraph of the letter:

> Dear Tam,
>
> Although this gift is arriving a little late, I must tell you that I felt it was important to send a knitted present. When I knit something, I think about the person or people for whom I am knitting with every stitch. There are thousands of stitches in this table runner and indeed, I did think about you and your family with every stitch.

In the box, I found the table runner and a copy of the *Livonia Observer* dated Thursday, December 4th, 1980. Glancing over the headlines throughout the newspaper, I found it remarkable that many of the same concerns appear in papers today. *Schools to Sue Over Stingy State Aid Plan* was on the front page along with *Students Seek Aid for Refugee Camp* and a picture of my family below it.

Looking at the portrait, I was reminded of what took place ten months before my parents' arrival in Michigan. They left Vietnam on January 13th, 1980 to escape from communism and in pursuit of freedom. On their journey to Thailand, their rickety boat narrowly survived an onslaught of heavy currents and thunderstorms. Even worse, the pirates from Thailand ransacked their boat, taking all of the women and leaving the men and children behind. Thankfully, they left my mother alone since she was pregnant with me, but she had to watch the other women in pain. A week later, the pirates returned the women back to their families, only to discover that all of the children had passed away. In quiet tears and embrace, my parents mourned the loss of their first-born son and nephew.

Once my parents arrived to the processing center in Thailand, they were scheduled to be transferred to the refugee camp in Songhkla. Australia, France, Germany, and Italy admitted those who had family residing in the country. America was the only country taking in refugees with no relatives. Those who fell in this category were sent to the same camp as my parents.

For the following months, each day mirrored itself with moments of eating and anticipating news of acceptance. Traveling in the same journey and living together created a sense of camaraderie amongst the refugees. Empathy allowed for them to deepen their relationship as they shared stories of their family in Vietnam and the ones lost along the way. Evenings would be filled with conversations about their dreams and how they look forward to a life with peace and simplicity. All of them chose to live from a stance of hope.

During my parents stay in Songkhla, my mother knitted sweaters for other refugees in the camp as a source of income. As for my father, he studied and practiced English in preparation for our move to America. In June, my parents welcomed my arrival and named me, "Tam," which means "compassion" in Vietnamese. They paired it with a middle name in dedication of my late older brother and together the name, "Minh Tam," means "pure soul."

A few weeks after I was born, my family received notice from the processing center that our paperwork had been misplaced. We were asked to relocate to Indonesia for further news of resettlement to America. Upon arriving to our next location, we were stationed at one of the barracks in Galang Island, where we were assigned a bunk bed with another family above us. My father continued to learn English and fetched water from the well on a daily basis. To make sure they had milk for me, my mother used the money she earned from knitting and bought bread to sell it to the rest of the refugees in the camp every morning.

The boredom and uncertainty of camp life created an undertone of unhappiness. At complete surrender, the speaker announced those who had received any letters and the names of people accepted for resettlement each day. For over three months, my parents experienced a whirlwind of emotions only to hear in October, "Vu Duc Hung…family of three." Immediately after the announcement, we rushed to the office to confirm the call and verify the documents. We were scheduled to depart to Michigan the weekend after Thanksgiving.

Upon arrival, our sponsors greeted us by the gate. The six months of planning and waiting had finally ended and the next challenge was finding a home for our family in Michigan. They worked together to find a place in the general area because of the two tentative job offers for my father. One was at the Plymouth Hilton Hotel and the other was custodial work with Livonia Public Schools. There was also a posting on the newspaper asking for clothing and donations to help cover living and medical expenses until we were adjusted. A handful of students from Franklin High School and their advisors, Ms. Peg Olson and Mr. John Rennels, came to our aid. Their generosity in time and effort has left my family in a debt of gratitude.

Before we were able to situate in a place of our own, Ms. Olson and her son, Matt, welcomed us into their home. They immersed my family into the American culture by exposing us to the food and customs. From Ms. Olson, we grew a liking for sloppy joes and donuts. We also learned common courtesy phrases such as "thank you" and "please." As for Mr. Rennels, he stopped by every morning to teach my father how to drive. Following each lesson, my parents took classes to learn English. Within a few weeks, my family felt a sense of community in Northville, Michigan.

After two cold winters, my mother and father were convinced to move to a warmer climate. In January of 1982, my family left to start a new beginning in California. We kept in touch with Mr. Rennels and Ms. Olson throughout the years by calling each other and writing letters. Over twenty years later, I took a trip to Michigan and reconnected with the both of them and their family in person.

As I look around at my family each time we gather, I often think about the love and generosity given to us from the students of Franklin High School, Mr. Rennels, Ms. Olson, and my parents. Through their actions, my brothers and I were given the opportunity to pursue our passion for service and most importantly, they gave us the freedom to create our own life. Each word woven into this story is a dedication to their kindness. Their love gives meaning and depth to this world by being examples of what it means to be life giving. They gave generously without expectation.

The journey my parents took upon themselves taught me a valuable lesson. Up until this day, they always mention about the wonderful people they met in Michigan. Although their experiences were difficult in Thailand, it was hardly discussed or a focus of our conversations growing up. My parents wanted to engrain with us the good things that came out of it and how kind and welcoming this world can be. They wanted us to live a life of gratitude and how a situation can be looked differently by the way we position our lens. It is what we learn and take action that matters in this lifetime.

Have you ever loved?

By: Glenn Xuan Long Hoa

Have u ever loved anyone
More than life itself?
More than freedom itself?

What would u give
For one last chance
To say to a departed one
"I love you", "I miss you", "Thank you".

The Boat People braved and faced death
Not to flee war - VN has been in war for centuries
Not to seek freedom - freedom is a state of mind
The Boat People braved and faced death
To give their descendants
A future.

The Boat People are a symbol
Of the Ultimate Sacrifice a parent can make,
Leaving behind
Everything they've ever worked for
Everything their parents ever worked for
Everything their ancestors ever worked for
For the hope
Of a future
For their children.

We are their children.
Let us honor their journey
Thank the countries that saved them from the sea
And build on their courage
To make this world
A better place to live.

Let's do this
Before
The Boat People depart.

Do it for your parents
Do it for your children
Do it for your loved ones
Do it selflessly.

Have u ever loved anyone
More than life itself?
More than freedom itself?

What would u give
For one last chance
To say to a departed one
"I love you", "I miss you", "Thank you".

Do it,
And do it now.

[Glenn Xuan Long Hoa is a dentist, born and raised in Montreal (province of Quebec, Canada. One of is surgical mentors, a Boat Person, told him his story. The man changed his life, as he suddenly realized that had he not survived his journey, Glenn wouldn't be who he was today.]

Captain Thach, Hero

[In preparing this book, I received an email from Captain James Van Thach that touched me deeply. Sometimes I forget there are heroes, Vietnamese and other ethnicities, still out there fighting to protect our freedoms. Thank you Captain Thach.]

Chao Anh Huy,

Here are two published news stories that I wrote with my cousin Anh Tommy about receiving a service dog to help with my injuries from the war in Iraq, and my return to the war zone in Afghanistan.

I have numerous severe injuries such as a brain injury and visual impaired blindness from the war and need assistance in typing, so these stories are in an interview setting. I'd like to contribute them as a Vietnamese-American to help fight against Terrorism, because of the great opportunities this country has provided my family when we arrived here as refugees.

The stories are below (edited).

1. Service Dog Given to Wounded Vietnamese-American U.S. Army Captain

As we honor the contributions of Asian-Pacific American Heritage month in the United States, a story that should be shared is of an Asian-American who has sacrificed so much for our country, Vietnamese-American United States Army Captain James Van Thach. Captain Thach walked away from a career as an aspiring lawyer when he graduated from Touro Law Center in 2002, after the terrorist attack on our country on September 11, 2001.

He deferred a career as an attorney in the military and requested to join the Infantry, which are land based soldiers specifically trained for the role of fighting on foot to engage the enemy face to face. Historically, the

Infantry has borne the brunt of the casualties of combat in wars to defend America," says Tommy Nero Sullivan of V.I.P. Promotions.

"After serving two arduous years in combat in Iraq, where the government of Iraq presented him the honorary rank of Staff Brigadier General and being twice wounded and earning the Purple Heart, Captain Thach now has a life filled with numerous medical appointments every month in the hope that he can have a manageable life, despite his injuries."

"I knew that I needed to do all that I can to help defend our country against terrorism before they can attempt to attack our country again," said Captain Thach.

"I learned from my Vietnamese heritage, for example as in South Vietnam, an enemy such as communist North Vietnam will violate the law and use terrorism to complete their goals to destroy a democratic nation."

"My relatives suffered and had to leave South Vietnam and immigrated to various counties such as the United States, Australia, Denmark and Holland. Our new adopted country of the United States had to be protected at all costs and there was not an alternative to change countries, because terrorism just like communism will follow anywhere to eradicate the democracy that we hold dear to our hearts," said Captain Thach.

Additionally Captain Thach said, "I am very fortunate that Canine Companions for Independence special program "Wounded Veterans Initiative" worked with my medical care team and matched me with my service dog Liz so that I can attain a greater control of the personal aspects of my daily activities."

2. Wounded U.S. Army Captain Goes to War Zone in Afghanistan

Why would an already wounded soldier return to the War Zone? Captain James Van Thach, retired from the United States Army in March 2009, decided it was time to return to a war zone on Operation Proper Exit, a program sponsored by the Troops First Foundation.

Captain Thach a Vietnamese American law graduate of Touro Law Center volunteered to serve in the Infantry and was wounded twice in Iraq, once by an Improvised Explosive Device (IED); second time by a Katyusha rocket and was awarded the Purple Heart for his wounds.

Since medically retiring from the United States Army, he has undergone physical and mental medical treatments for the numerous injuries that he sustained: Traumatic Brain Injury, migraine headaches, photophobia, diplopia, blurred vision, sciatic nerve damage to left leg, injury to his neck, back and spine and Post Traumatic Stress Disorder (PTSD).

"When I returned from the Iraq War to the United States and received treatment, my health has gone up and down several times which has lead me to be admitted into the hospital several times," said Captain Thach.

"After three long years my health finally stabilized. After watching a CBS 60 Minutes story about Troops First Foundation that was providing a trip called Operation Proper Exit for wounded Veterans returning to Iraq, I felt that this was for me to receive final closure," said Captain Thach.

In December 2011, the United States military's combat role in Iraq ended and Captain Thach was not able to return there. His doctor agreed that it would benefit him to go on Operation Proper Exit and help to heal his mental scars, anxiety attacks, depression, hyper vigilance and nightmares which still linger on after more than 3 years. As long as he took his daily dosage of 20 pills and was injected with his bi-weekly injection before he left, going to the war zone in Afghanistan would be tremendously advantageous for him.

Captain Thach said, "Operation Proper Exit has helped me tremendously going into the war zone in Afghanistan with 8 other Veterans that have been wounded. We formed a brotherhood and interacted with troops throughout Afghanistan, shared our stories of our wounds and how we persevered and moved on with our lives despite our injuries."

In conclusion, Captain Thach stated, "Our injuries don't define us. We control our own destinies and set the example on how to live our lives positively and be inspirational to our fellow Americans as well as an asset to our country."

Captain Thach, your bravery to return to a dangerous war zone in Afghanistan despite your debilitating injuries speaks volumes about your character. You are a shining light of what makes our country great, we are forever in your debt for your sacrifice.

Chapter 10: Quê Hương
(Homecoming)

This chapter deals with Vietnamese overseas coming back to Vietnam and their experiences.

A Preface: All I Hope to Do in Lists

by: Angeline Mai-Anh Vuong

A passport to fill with travel stamps.
A sturdy 45 liter multi-use backpack.
Notebooks for thoughts and verbiage.
An open spirit for wanderlust.

Check.

I sit in this crowded, now transformed abode (once called my bedroom) with clothes strewn, shoes thrown, and papers upon endless papers piled high. Even though some closest to me say that I am the epitome of a very judicious planner (OCD even), this is different. The chaos of this upcoming is different from any other trip or move I have made or possibly will make in the future.

There is an ache. An ache to understand, to connect, to learn. But with that desire is the very real anxiety of moving to a country that has held so much pain and distress for those who have made sacrifices so that I could be alive today. *Tại sao con muốn trở lại nơi mà Ba Mẹ đã từng rang rời khỏi?* It is in that ache, that houses the want of exploring a place I call quê hương. A landscape with endless cobbled paths, odiferous smells of phở gà, and clear azure ocean amidst fog capped mountain ranges. Vietnam. You are the land in my dreams.

It's funny when you know you want something. You either giggle with a simple mention of the idea or find reasons to justify this need. My motivation for moving to Vietnam is an indefinable, nebulous affair of the heart and mind. A decidedly work-in-progress shall I say. A treatise perhaps of selfish intrigue and a human need to explore. Despite the explained (or unexplained) excuses of the past few months to begin this adventure—to start a more democratic revolution (jokingly), to reconnect with my culture and a burgeoning generation, to re-enter the space of international policymaking, to learn the culinary secrets from old grandmothers, to empower women in their pursuit of education and opportunities to thrive—none of them compare to the very real and fascinating subjects I call Ba Me. It will and always will be about the spectacled dentist with a mischievous smile, and the demure lady with an air of elegance and soft spoken nature. When I think of them, my heart swells with affection and profound awe. It is because of their story that I want to shape my own future. They will probably never understand my need to do this, but in the end, it is my tapestry to craft.

I want my story to be a story about strength and acknowledgement. Of gratitude for their resilience and sacrifices, but also a quest to follow my own compass. I want this to be a treatise of my personal growth and cultural self-discovery more so than my professional development. I want this to be a history lesson of which I am both the student and teacher. I want this to be an opportunity to recognize the privilege of being a Vietnamese American woman. I want to take risks and be open to endless opportunities. I want to appreciate freedom. I want to find purpose and meaning. I want to trust.

Memoirs are our love letters and our letters of apologies. They hold our few gems, the noteworthy lessons of our journeys. So here begins my journey. Cheers to the sublime with an inquisitive and intrepid spirit. What better place than home?

[Angeline is small but mighty. She is the Chairwoman of BPSOS, an international Vietnamese non-profit, a Board Member of the Youth Leadership Council, and has been part of many political campaigns. Angeline is a strong

supporter of the Trinity University Tigers and the Cal-Berkley Bears]

Full Circle; Growing up

By: Ngoc Anh Nguyen

You know that feeling you get when you visit your high school after graduating, and everything just seems so small? I had that feeling (amplified a thousand fold) when I visited the home I grew up in last Tet. I grew up in a very small home with my entire extended family on the outskirts of Saigon. My grandmother, aunts, uncles, cousins, parents and I all inhabited that house for the first seven years of my life. It was more than enough for me. I remember laying out reading books on the top floor as my mom hung laundry to dry. I remember scooching on my bottom down the stairs each morning for breakfast. We had a small toilet in the backyard (aka hole in the ground) which I assumed was pretty standard!

Last Tet I took my Jewish fiancé back to that home where my aunts and cousins still live. My grandmother has since passed away. Children have grown up and moved out, and started having children themselves. Some children were born and live there now. The house just seemed so small. The once massive living room that hosted many parties seemed crowded with four Americans sitting on the couch. I stifled a chuckle as I watched my 200+lb fiancé squeeze on a plastic stool around a small table eating canh, cơm chiên, and thịt kho to celebrate the New Year. My aunts were eager to show off their cooking and kept telling us to eat! eat! while giggling at my fiancé's sign language and attempts at communication.

I wondered how he must see my house, my family members, my very meager beginnings. Later that night, I asked him how the experience was. To my pleasant surprise, he loved his time in my house. Not only seeing where I came from, but feeling the warmth and hospitality of my family members made him feel like he got to know me on a deeper level.

I felt proud. I felt proud of where I came from, no matter how small it seemed. I felt proud that I've retained these values of humility, hospitality, and kindness. I've come a long way since I've moved to America, but I wouldn't give up those years I spent in Vietnam for the world. The Vietnamese are a proud people. We work hard, and we care for those around us. Our people have taken these skills and values to the United States and have succeeded tremendously. I'm grateful my parents raised me the way they did, and that's what it means to me to be a Vietnamese-American.

[Ngoc Anh is a graduate of Rice University and the Baylor School of Medicine. She works as an Emergency Room Physician. She and her fiancé also regularly kick my butt in tennis.]

More Vietnamese than I think

By: Kyle Le

I shoveled tiny clams mixed with rice into my mouth and wondered how someone could ever de-shell these hến enough to pile their flesh on a mountain of a plate that was in front of me. The sun finally began to make its descent, and the masses will surely thank it for doing so on this particularly scorching day. Despite sweating my weight in water in the unforgiving afternoon heat of Central Vietnam, this meal alone proved worthy of the lengthy journey from So Cal to Saigon and finally to Hoi An. I asked for the bill, paid, stood up, and noticed the remaining grains of rice left in my bowl. I couldn't help but think of my mom 8,000 miles away and how she nagged at me for leaving left over rice which will eventually turn into maggots awaiting for me in hell.

I'm more Vietnamese than I think.

I spotted a stream of smoke and a boy behind a rock burning joss paper. I joked with him about how he's going to get burned if he plays with fire. He stared at me blankly and smiled. Some things just get lost in translation. I used to be embarrassed when my dad would burn joss paper in the backyard after another ceremony that involved waiting for the incense to burn out as the food got cold when the spirits unfairly got first dibs. I would hurry and rush him to finish. I was certain neighbors wouldn't understand and probably thought we were either engaging in some cult activity or had a barbeque and didn't invite them. I squatted next to the boy as he began to light gold bars on fire. I started to help him, and we threw money silently into the flames just like my dad and I on cold nights hovering over that old paint bucket blackened to a crisp. Nowadays, I wish embers wouldn't die so quickly.

I approached a large crowd of bystanders with their attention fixated around a circle. So naturally, my curiosities lead me toward the commotion. A group of young teenagers sporting fitted and snapback caps danced to the tune of a generic hip hop beat with the 500-year-old Japanese Bridge in the background. They taped pieces of cardboard together on the ground and used it to protect their heads and limbs when they attempted to emulate the moves they saw in movies. I caught a glimpse of my cousin Duke in them momentarily and how he used to film videos of himself dancing to similar beats. They seemed to be around his age too, yet despite all the differences at the end of the day if I threw Duke in the middle of this crowd and onto the makeshift dance floor, he would surely blend right in with these youths. Despite barely being able to speak Vietnamese, despite his citizenship, and despite cultural barriers that we're all familiar with, at the end of the day Duke is still ethnically a Vietnamese teenager. One day he'll realize this. And I wish someone had told me this when I was a teenager.

I sat down on a straw mat and bobbed my head to the sounds of folk music sung in a popular bingo game that plays nightly in the heart of the old town. I couldn't help but sway along. The same singers shared the stage with each other just like four years ago when I first visited this place. And just like that time, I was at such peace and enjoyment hearing the blaring voices screeching out of the speakers next to me. To some, traditional Vietnamese music could resemble ear deafening torture. However, the current me can't get enough of it. Cải lương was featured heavily in my childhood, thanks to my mother. It was a guilty pleasure that I was too ashamed to admit because anything Vietnamese wasn't considered cool with my friends then. My mom used to blast Vũ Linh and Kim Tử Long in the car whenever she dropped me off at school. Each day I begged her to turn it down, but as I got out, she would just turn it up to humble me. Many years down the road, I enthusiastically blasted all sorts of loud classical Asian music in my car all over town. I can feel the sounds of the gongs in my subwoofer rattling my trunk. And now, sitting and hearing the same instrumentals played in the background only brought me closer to the past and the realization that my fondness for the stage and art came because while other kids were watching Sesame Street, I was watching cải lương with my mom.

A small kerosene lamp placed on a rounded woven basket illuminated some chairs surrounding an old woman came to view, and without any signage, I still knew exactly what I was getting myself into. Hột vịt lộn, !@$% Yeah! I sat down on a plastic stool fit for a toddler, and asked for a couple of eggs to start. The woman gently lifted the cover from a basket and dug out some eggs and placed them delicately on a small plate with chipped edges. She added a tiny teacup, a handful of rau răm, salt, chilies, and a green kumquat with the head cut off. I cracked the rounder end with a spoon, gently peeled away at the shell enough to break the skin-like layer, and the juices that came out were magical. I simply feasted ravenously and remembered how all these years my cravings for balut eggs never halted. I know it goes against western culture to say that I enjoy eating baby duck embryos, but I can't help it. I enjoy eating baby duck embryos. I remember long drives to the Vietnamese supermarket and smelling the fresh, but not too fresh produce. It's something you can't smell at an Albertsons for sure. I would go to the cereal section wanting to buy the latest one I saw on TV. Usually, the selections were either too limited there or my mom would trump my decision and claim that a particular kind was too nóng because supposedly chocolate makes you hot. But she never said no to balut eggs. Other families would go out on a Sunday and eat Burger King together, but my family ate baby ducks together.

Hoi An closes early. By 10 o' clock or so, most shops are boarded up, and the last remaining staggering tourists make their way back to their hotels. I wandered the streets for a bit, gazing into dimly lit alleys, not wanting the night to end. Every western tourist that passed me felt like a foreigner to me. Every Vietnamese local that passed me reflected like a family member I knew. And despite the current distance and ocean between us now, thanks to my parents, and thanks to Vietnam, I am who I am today. And I'm so proud of that.

[Kyle is an American Viet Kieu living in Vietnam. He manages the popular blog http://www.kylele.net as well as the popular YouTube channel SoJournaling Vietnam at https://www.youtube.com/user/kyleledotnet.]

My Shelter

By: Ai Vuong

My children's shelter was a different place back then. When I first arrived, blue suitcases dragging behind I walked through the iron blue gates, thirty two pairs of eyes were assessing me. They were judging me and I knew it. They were used to volunteers. An air of suspicion clung to the air as their eyes followed me as I navigated around the hallways and rooms. Hundreds had come before. While each volunteer was special, in the end, after a few days, weeks, or months, they eventually left. I thought that after my volunteer commitment was up, I too, would say goodbye.

I came to Huế at the end of the summer of 2009 and the original plan was to be there for one year. I decided to volunteer in Vietnam because I wanted to spend the year "helping people," but truly I wanted time to figure out what I was to do with "the rest of my life." I was only going to be here for a year; this was only going to be rest stop for the all the other places I was meant to be, I had assured my family and myself. The first stop was Huế, where I posted to this particular children's shelter. My job description consisted of living at the shelter, teaching English, and assisting in any other tasks assigned by the staff. The job seemed simple enough, and I was ready for "work."

This was just my job for the next year, and then I could leave. That year passed slowly, and at times, painfully. I had always prided myself in being so "Vietnamese" when in fact, I was more "American" than I had ever imagined. When I needed personal space, I always walked into my room to find at least five kids littered in each corner. When I needed words of comfort, I never understood the heavy Central region dialect and ended up just nodding along to empty conversations. In my arrogance, I thought living at the shelter would be easy because I knew Vietnamese culture and had an exit plan. It was in reality so much harder than I had ever anticipated, sometimes so utterly lonely I would lie in bed and cry at night. I really didn't understand anything, not the language, not the culture, and especially not the work. I tried to hide my tears from the 32 kids at the time, but I think they knew. You can't hide anything from children - their hearts are so pure and their eyes so piercing. They love you only as you love them, and did I ever learn to love them.

Loving for me was hard at the time. My father, he had the heaviest heart of any man I'd ever known. My mother, she had the thickest skin. My mom left our house when I was fourteen, and when she did, that place no longer was home. She left for reasons I was too young to understand now, and probably still am. All I knew then was that she wasn't there anymore. My mom never loved me in the way I wanted or craved for her to, with gifts instead of time, but I can't deny that she loved me just as deeply. My dad, though, loved me in the way that I needed, pulling out his hair day after day raising my little brother and me after my mom left, but something was taken away from him that I don't think he ever got back. His fire burned out long ago.

I was so angry at them then, so bitter. I couldn't understand why she left, nor could I understand why he couldn't stop being depressed, so I reacted the only way I could at the time. I left. I ran away to Vietnam to find myself. Or rather, I left to find them again a country they ran away from so many years ago.

What I found were these children. It turned out I needed them more than they could ever need me. I needed them to hug me, to hold me, to take care of me. We needed each other just at the right time.

But the shelter then was a difficult place to live, for both the children and me.

"This place is like a prison," Nhật confided in me one late night when we had the rare opportunity to speak alone. He was a good kid, but misunderstood. Someone was stealing items at the shelter, and all fingers were pointed at him. He had stolen a few things before. Unfortunately, one bad behavior or one bad action equated to a "broken" child. Because he had stolen once, he was forever labeled as a "stealer." He seemed to be the obvious culprit. It wasn't difficult to blame each other for missing items; there were 32 kids and 6 staff members occupying a two-story building. There was no privacy. But there was also no trust. The staff blamed the kids, the kids blamed each other.

These kids didn't feel like this shelter was their home, and neither did I. The shelter had been having much staff turnover for the past few years, and rumors and gossip pervaded a place which was supposed to be home. Someone would whisper something to someone else, and fast as any wild fire assumptions would become truth. There was gossip of money laundering or of stealing or of plotting to gain power. These may sound like inconsequential rumors, and I'll never know the truth to any of the gossip, but the reality at the moment was that the kids were the ones suffering. They didn't trust anyone, particularly not the adults who were there to protect them and love them. I wanted to protect them from it, from the pain and hurt they felt here, but I had no idea what to do as a volunteer. This wasn't my job.

Maybe I wasn't meant to do anything. One Saturday night on my way to meet up with some friends, eager to escape the shelter, I found Hương hiding alone, her shadow cast along the empty hallway. I had always felt drawn to her because she, too, was misunderstood. Most times she would shrug it off and laugh loudly. She showed her teeth when she smiled, vastly different from other traditional Huế girls who always covered, with a genteel hand, their even more genteel smile. This day, I walked up behind her and found her crying. She asked me why people always teased her, especially at the shelter? My heart broke yet again at that moment. All I could do then was wrap my arm around her and cry with her. She healed me, though, when she said, "Cám ơn, Mẹ."

It was then that I knew. I had run away from my parents, but I was running desperately towards these kids. Angry or bitter as I was, I was turning my back towards my own parents' love and affection. These kids didn't have that option. Maybe I couldn't do anything, but the least I could do was love them in the way that they needed.

I was close to giving up, though. I couldn't take the rumors, the gossip, and the mistrust. I lost hope in this place.

It wasn't until Jenny Do, the Chairwoman, came back to the shelter in December of 2010 that my life changed. I don't know what she saw in me, but she entrusted her shelter, and her children to me. She named me the Deputy Director.

"View them like they're your kids, Ai. This is *your* shelter," she told me, looking deeply into my eyes. She said she could look into my heart, see my soul, and she's making the right decision. Don't I dare let her down.

But, what if I did? Could I handle the lives of all these children on my shoulders? Could I accept this responsibility? I was 24. I didn't even know what the hell I was doing with my life. Could I do this?

I had no idea how to go about changing the situation there, but I knew I had to lead with love. I, along with so many others who loved and believed in the shelter, began to instill positive youth development and positive psychology practices. We only talked about strengths, not deficiencies. We talked about dreams. We asked the kids not only to dream, but to dream big.

And oh, their dreams are grand. My kids have done things they've never thought they had the capability to do. One summer, they became photographers and held a photo exhibition entitled "A World Through Different Lens" with a group of volunteers from Monta Vista High School in California. For three consecutive summers, groups of the kids went on a volunteer service trip to help build schools with Sunflower Mission. They then returned to the shelter to create their own community service projects. The kids would then get on stage at our large community events to present their projects. The courage and ability for these kids at 12, 13, or 14 years old to stand up in front of a large crowd and tell their stories is beyond my comprehension. It's through their spirit and their accomplishments that the shelter began to heal. The kids breathed life back into this place — their dreams filled the shelter.

This summer of 2014 marks my fifth year here, with my kids and I piloting a leadership program together for other youth in our community. What could happen when these kids, who previously have been provided so many opportunities, are the ones to give back to their community? The results have been amazing. My kids, who just a few years ago, underestimated their talents, are the ones leading, coaching, and training other children to, above all, believe in their own strengths and capabilities and most importantly, love each other. These kids have come so far.

Five years ago, I was a different person, too. Then, I was running away from my family. Mom, Dad, I'm sorry I had lied to you all those years earlier when I said I'd only go to Việtnam for just one year. I had really believed myself, then. I was foolish to think Việtnam was a pause on the road to the rest of my life, only a step towards all that I was meant to be. My "something big" is this — right here, right now.

My kids and I. Our lives are intertwined, fated in a way I can only comprehend as duyên nợ. I want to be with them as long as I can. In my heart of hearts I know this has always been exactly where I was meant to be and what I was meant to do.

This job is the best job in the world if it means I get to love these kids with all that I've got, and in them, I have a home. I'm not going anywhere.

[Ai Vuong is the executive director of Friends of Hue (http://www.friendsofhue.org). She's a proud Texas longhorn alum, and recently received her Masters of Public Administration from NYU. As the ED of Friends of Hue, she is focuses on youth development, leadership training, critical service learning and ultimately, sustainability. She's also wickedly funny and an excellent writer.]

The Squid Sellers of Sihanoukville

By: Andrew X. Pham

On the long white beaches of Sihanoukville, yoke-basket women trudge across the hot, blinding sand, their silhouettes etched against a shimmering sea. They shield their faces from the tropical sun with palm hats and their limbs with long-sleeve blouses and pants. They look as if they have just walked out of the rice paddies. Scintillating aromas of grilled squids waft from their swaying baskets. They are the humble purveyors of the tastiest morsels in this Cambodian seaside resort.

The squids they sell have been caught fresh a few miles from shore, mere hours ago. Last night, the fishermen steered their illuminated boats out towards the deep water. One could see them from the beach, bright green dots stretched across the night horizon like a string of Christmas lights. By the predawn hours, their catch was ashore, sorted, iced, and on the way to market. By noon, these women were barbecuing little kebabs for beachgoers.

The squids are at once delectable and crude, similar to what I ate at fishermen's bonfires as a boy. There is no preparation to speak of, the women simply skewer them whole—tentacles, arms, beak, gut, and gladius, full with the sea's brininess—on bamboo sticks, baste them with a sweet-spicy-sour sauce, and grill them over coals. Within a few short minutes, hot juices bubble out of these thumb-size "sea sausages" and sizzle on the glowing coals, tantalizing the senses. Served with a side of the tangy sauce, one US dollar for five. Irresistible with ice-cold beers, heavenly after a swim!

As someone who has spent most of his life by the sea, I have an innate affinity for fresh seafood and a penchant for settling in seaside towns with a bustling fish market, particularly those on the oceans of Southeast Asia. Born in a Vietnamese fishing village, I've traveled the coast from northern Vietnam to Cambodia, Thailand, Malaysia, all the way to Singapore, and have dined in fishing villages all along the way. Sihanoukville is definitely a stellar seafood destination. Other places might have greater varieties of seafood, even at lower prices, but I've found no vendors, anywhere, like the Sihanoukville vendors. That is to say, I find these vendors even more remarkable than the squids.

These compact women, who remind me of my own grandmothers years ago, are not, as one might expect, from Sihanoukville—nor are they even Cambodian. I overhear them talking among themselves in Viet, with the heavy, flat southern accent. When I inquire about their *que* (birth village), most gesture eastward to Chau Doc, a port town on the Cambodian border. They have left home and journeyed to a neighboring country for the small privilege of selling tidbits of food from their yoke-baskets. For a moment, I wonder unreasonably if Bao, my long-lost childhood friend, might be among them—a reflex or, perhaps, an affliction of trauma. So, day after day, for weeks on end, I gravitate to the beach to eat grilled squids and to hear their stories.

To understand how these Vietnamese women came to sell grilled squids on this remote Cambodian shore is to cast a long gaze down the decades through the lens of social economics and history of Southeast Asia.

The American-Vietnam War scattered my people all over Southeast Asia. Pockets of Vietnamese could be found a thousand kilometers outside the country in every direction. Their foods survived the migration and lingered for generations, even after their mother tongue faded and their culture was all but absorbed by the host country. Today, it's possible to eat *pho* in the Philippines, *canh ca chua* in Indonesia, *banh cuon* in Singapore, *banh mi* in Thailand, and *com phan* in Laos.

After the Vietnamese army ended the Khmer Rouge rule in 1979, Sihanoukville became a natural destination for a number of southern Vietnamese refugees because it sat along the same coast, about a hundred kilometers as the crow flies from the border. Many crossed into Cambodia on foot, trekking through the jungle. Most continued onward, overland to Thailand, in hope of finding passage to America, Australia, or Europe. A few stayed and established new lives in Cambodia. More came by small fishing boats, some accidentally washed ashore by storms, others intentionally beached on Cambodian shores to avoid the vicious Thai and Malay pirates who plundered, raped, and murdered thousands of Vietnamese with impunity in the Gulf of Thailand.

My own family embarked on this same voyage, thirty-seven years ago, with full knowledge of the perils awaiting us at sea. The storm winds of Fate blew us off course, away from the Gulf of Thailand, and sank us in a shipping lane in the South China Sea. In our direst hours, a Russian ship followed us from afar, and a

French ship passed within shouting distance but did not offer assistance or supplies. An Indonesian freighter, under the command of a Captain Matapukan, saved my family, plucking us from the tossing sea as our fishing vessel disintegrated beneath our feet. (We and our descendants shall remember and honor his name.)

When Vietnam opened its market and eased travel restrictions in the mid 1990s, Vietnamese in Cambodia began returning to visit their families and establish trade. After the Indian Ocean Tsunami of December 2004 decimated tourist traffic in the Andaman Ocean, Sihanoukville entered a period of rapid growth which continues to the current day. Rising prices and long-term visa restrictions in Thailand also spurred Western expats and foreign companies to relocate to Cambodia. With sharp economic growth, the Vietnamese expats began recruiting and bringing their relatives and countrymen to work in Sihanoukville.

The squid sellers are among the recent arrivals as part of a large contingent of food-basket vendors, nearly all women and children, who sell sunglasses, woven bracelets, fruits, boiled quail eggs, fried rock lobsters, noodle soup, papaya salad, grilled chicken wings, sausages, and other types of seafood—a portion of which are purchased by Vietnamese and Cambodian workers (they need to eat too). Some have set up permanent homes in Sihanoukville, while others choose to work here during the high season and return to Vietnam during the brief low season when the monsoon sweeps away foreign tourists save the rare Middle Easterners who come specifically for the rain.

After I've planted myself in the same spot on the beach for a week, one vendor claims me as one of her regulars. In her early forties, Loan Nguyen arrived in Sihanoukville the previous year with her entire family. Her husband works in construction. Her twelve-year-old daughter sells fruits on the beach with her. Her six-year-old son is in a makeshift daycare-school set up by Vietnamese women in the Viet shanty. They are part of a large group who seek to put roots down in Cambodia because opportunities back home are too scarce.

I ask her why not try Vung Tau, Nha Trang, or other resort towns in Vietnam. She dismisses that with a wry smile and replies in Viet, *"It's too competitive in those beach towns. The locals there do not want outsiders invading their territory. Vietnam has too many people. No matter what we do, it's very hard for landless people like us to make a living in Vietnam. My husband and I worked in factories, on a shrimp farm, and on construction crews, but we barely made enough to eat. We lived day-to-day. We couldn't afford the books and school fees for our children. The day our strength fails is the day we go hungry. There is no hope, no future in that kind of work."*

Thirty-seven years ago, Loan's father was sent to a re-education camp as punishment for his military service as a sergeant in the South Vietnamese Army during the War. (My father suffered the same sentence.) After his release, the Communists confiscated his home and sent him and his family into the jungle to farm. They were officially marked for systemic discrimination that barred them from higher education and good jobs. Thus began their lifetime of poverty and deprivation, which extended to their children and grandchildren.

Her story is one I know well because it is a life my own family narrowly escaped. We have friends and relatives who did not elude this fate. My childhood friend Bao and his family were sent to the jungle, never to be seen again.

Thousands of impoverished Vietnamese have been flocking to Cambodia, alone or with family in tow, in search of work. Many consider themselves fortunate to be able to work without being separated from their loved ones. If they need to return to Vietnam, the border is only a day's bus ride away. People like Loan, who carry scars and grudges against the Vietnamese Communists, are not looking back. They stake their dreams and future in Cambodia, a country poorer and less developed than their motherland.

Over long lazy afternoons on the beach, I make the acquaintance of Loan and her vendor friends. I come to view their life stories as possible scenarios for my own had we not escaped Vietnam. They ask about my *que* and how my family "crossed the border." Once word gets out that I am the Viet-kieu who translated the diaries of Dr. Tram Thuy, vendors begin stopping by to share their stories. All consider themselves to be more free than the Vietnamese women who married aging Korean farmers (through match-making agencies) to endure lonely lives of agricultural drudgery in a cold, foreign country. They count themselves more fortunate than those who have signed crushing labor contracts—a modern form of enslavement—to work in Korea, Japan, and even Russia. These desperate people have scrounged money from relatives or borrowed from loan sharks for the agent fees and airfares to go abroad to work in industrial sweatshops, to live confined in filthy dormitories without rights or protection from abuse.

Their realities seem at odds with Vietnam's image as a country of rapid progress and much-touted economic prowess. While Vietnam's GDP (nominal, per capita) leads those of Cambodia and Laos by decent margins, it still lags behind Thailand's by a factor of five. Viewed in conjunction with population density data, the real picture emerges. Vietnam is twice as densely populated as Thailand, three times more than Cambodia, and ten times more than Laos. In other words, a poor Cambodian may earn 30% less income than his Vietnamese counterpart, but the Cambodian may also have three times more land with which he might be able to grow just enough food to feed himself and his family. It's a little known fact: Vietnam has an extremely poor and desperate underclass that is willing to go anywhere and accept any amount of risk to earn a living.

Loan says, *"Vietnamese tourists, Saigon people, come here. They're surprised to see us working in Sihanoukville, but they don't ask too many questions. They know how hard life is for the poor in Vietnam."*

My great grandaunt used to say: *A rich man is blind to a beggar's hunger until he sees him eat the table scraps left out for dogs.* I find myself fumbling with explanations for the disparities between our worlds, saying such triteness as there are no borders in heaven and how we will all be reborn in different skins in different countries.

Loan pats my forearm. *"Only Heavens knows Destiny."*

On my last day in Sihanoukville, Loan treats me to a free plate of large grilled squids. They are every bit as delicious as the first squids I enjoyed on this beach, but they have also acquired new dimensions. At moments, I have difficulties swallowing.

For survivors, the food of memories can turn suddenly bitter or sweet in the mouth. Sometimes, they burn like fire.

[Andrew is an author, critic, travel writer, rice farmer, and engineer. He lives and writes from a wooden bungalow he built on the Mekong River. He lives to eat. He exercises to eat more. Andrew is the author of Catfish and Mandala: A Two-Wheeled Voyage Through the Landscape and Memory of Vietnam (1999) and The Eaves of Heaven: A Life in Three Wars (2009). He is also the translator of Last Night I Dreamed of Peace (2008).]

Chinese-Vietnamese Identity

By: Francesca Huynh

There I was, propped on the back of a dusty, cackling moped, thrusting my hands into the air like some kid on a rollercoaster ride. I was speeding down the roads of Ho Chi Minh City at night with my cousin, feeling the wind crash against my face and watching storefronts blur into lights and colors. It was the most unexpected form of harmony: the unified circling of the mopeds, the sweet smells of grilled sticky rice, and the dazzling flower-shaped lights together shared a story of Vietnam that was equally exhilarating and comforting. At that moment, nothing else mattered but this great sense of euphoria. I knew that when I returned to New York City and sat down to record this very moment, this memory would be my connection to Vietnam, a place that once felt distant, mysterious, and foreign.

It was my first trip to my parents' homeland. In traveling to Vietnam for a month, I was not looking for just a vacation, but also an understanding of the country my parents so lovingly called home and a chance to connect 20 years of stories with faces and places. For my mother, it was almost the same case. Having not been back in ten years, Vietnam in many ways was like visiting a new place. We were both tourists in a country we thought we knew so much about.

For as long as my mother told me her stories of growing up during the Vietnam War, I knew them, could recite them, but did not truly understand them. And for a long time, I was confused about my own identity. I was not born Vietnamese; my Chinese parents were born and raised in Vietnam, while I was born in America. Even though I was not technically Vietnamese, I never felt like I wasn't in Vietnam—I baked in the sun with all the moped riders, sat with locals on the side of the road for delicious but unhygienic food, and spent countless hours sitting with my family and listening to new and old tales.

Growing up with just my parents in Boston, I never had the opportunity to bond with a large extended family. When my friends spoke of festive family gatherings—however dysfunctional they were—I secretly envied them. The long Thanksgiving dinner table (hot pot version of course) was never quite reality for me. As the first generation born in America, I am forever grateful for the life my parents provided for me, as lonely as it may have seemed at times. Every time we sat down for our humble Thanksgiving meal, talking about the past and the present, I found myself longing for family. So to look for my family, I turned to my parents' past in Vietnam to learn more about the people who shaped my parents' lives and ultimately, my own.

My bedtime stories were a little unconventional to say the least. Instead of hares and turtles, I listened in awe to bold stories of escape and freedom. I heard them all: from the stories of the Vietnamese boat people to my mother's early entrepreneurial spirit selling beef jerky at Saigon's outdoor marketplaces to raise money to leave the war-ridden country. Like any other child, I nagged her for more stories. I tried to imagine their stories in my head by attending to every detail, so I could not just know those stories but feel them. Those stories, however close they may feel, were still distant. Last January those words and those stories finally became alive, retold in full illustration. Buzzing around Vietnam, I was as much a part of those stories as I was the creator of new ones.

On my long flight back to America, I realized that I am as much Vietnamese as I am Chinese or American and by exploring my parents' past, I am learning to slowly piece together my heritage. Wherever my future takes me, I promise to engage not just the history behind the ancient landmarks, but how my life and my past can be found in those places too. I will come home armed with stories to tell my parents in return one day. No matter my destination, I hope to experience stories and adventures as magical and magnificent as that night ride in Vietnam.

[Francesca is the Associate Director for the New York City Asian American Student Conference (NYCAASC. She is working on an independent project about the Chinese-Vietnamese Identity (focusing on the 1st and 2nd generation ethnic Chinese from Vietnam) found at: http://www.chinesevietnamese.com.]

Việt Kiều

By: Jennifer Vi Nguyen

———

"Nếu mà có nhiều tiền, mẹ đi du lịch ở đâu?"

"If you had all the money in the world, where would you go?"

———

My host mother knew that the Việt Kiều, with the strut and sway of their plumper, American bodies, could be spotted from a considerable distance. Even before the intricate tapestry of their attire came into view, even before they opened their mouths, even before they let out the wavering tone of their regurgitated Vietnamese, the Saigonese could detect the sight, the scent, the sensation of a Vietnamese American. My host mother knew that despite my newly acquired tan, I still spoke like a Vietnamese cave man, flinched as I walked directly into incoming traffic, and solicited a "hello" rather than a "chào" as I passed opened doors to opened houses in the neighborhood. So she carried my American passport to the nearest police station, slipped the officers a few thousand Vietnamese đồng for their afternoon cup of cà phê, and informed the neighborhood that Jennifer Nguyen need not be reported – she was neither kidnapped nor lost, but merely a guest in the Huyền household, an American student studying Vietnamese.

My host mother knew how to appease my diluted Việt Kiều palette, how to perfectly grill thịt nướng, letting the pork sweeten and lightly char over a bed of covered coals. She knew the ideal proportion of prawns to rice flour for bánh xèo, flipping, folding, and frying the crepe until it crackled and illuminated a yellow unfamiliar to my American eyes. She knew that each cooking session required the dipping of chả giò into peanut oil, crisping the egg rolls until the skin became golden and glistened. She knew that if the fish sauce was too pungent, the fried frog legs too terrifying, or the hot and sour soup too hot and/or too sour, she could rely on the universal appeal of the egg roll to appease my fickle appetite.

My host mother knew how to cram my stockpile of Vietnamese purchases into a small box, packing the assorted shapes into a space that could barely contain a bag of rice. She cushioned the tall, "Saigon Bia" emblazoned glasses with orange rags, placing them among the cans of Ba Ba Ba, Tiger, and Saigon Select. The arrangement prevented a disastrous explosion of Vietnamese alcohol as it traveled across the pacific. Her careful gestures shatter-proofed the memory of my towering over the customers at the Co-Op Mart as held beer and nothing else – an amusement for the female cashier, a gift for my father. The comics featuring a Vietnamese Tin Tin defeating the Chinese were deftly stacked and sandwiched between the cook books and Vietnamese-English dictionaries, awaiting a much anticipated reading by my mother. The oversized, imitation designer polos covered the pirated Hollywood movies, the pairs of wooden chopsticks, the sixteen feathered shuttlecocks, and the other purchases made with a mere pointing, pleading, and passing of paper đồng. The 30 pound, 13.6 kilogram package was tightly wrapped in packing tape, stickered, marked, and placed on a boat where it floated in the Pacific Ocean for three months, bound for a red brick house in Texas.

My host mother knew the history of her Thủ Đức, her district of Saigon, her fragment of Vietnam. She walked me through the open-air markets where the green leaves of rau dripped with beads of water, where the dragon fruit was an alien shade of magenta, where the air mixed of earth, exhaust, and the fragrance of warm French bread. She guided me through the city center, maneuvering her motorbike through crowds and dried squid vendors as she leisurely described the post office, the school, and the hospital. She singled out her international cong ty where she worked in the newly-erected business park – a series of plain metal structures where the Vietnamese manufactured and assembled shoes, pillows, and electronics for the British, the Japanese and the Americans. In a small cove inside of her factory, my host mother worked for the Koreans, mixing traditional medicines and remedies for sick Vietnamese workers.

My host mother knew how to tend to dog bites, diagnose dengue fever, and soothe all that ailed my wheezing, foreign immune system. But, what she did not know came in the form of an answer to my curious, dessert conversation question:

"Nếu mà có nhiều tiền, mẹ đi du lịch ở đâu?" I asked in my hesitant, new language, curious about her traveling ambitions.

Surprised, she paused, a motionless knife in one hand, a half-peeled fruit in the other.

"I don't know," she replied in Vietnamese. "I never really thought about it."

―――――――

The first thing I learned in Vietnamese class was how to say my name. From the corner of Vietnam National University's Thủ Đức library, the chorus of Americans echoing "Tôi tên là" filled the empty spaces between the Vietnamese history books and the TOEFL guides. By midday, the stifling humidity of Saigon seeped into the room as we tediously fumbled through our respective introductions. The lone fan would loudly sway from left to right, doing little to relieve the oppression in returning the assaulting heat at a higher, more concentrated velocity. "Tôi tên là" we would utter, five of six nodding off from the bullets of hot air. My mouth drooped, battling the boil and the boredom of already knowing my name in English and in Vietnamese.

Overwhelmed by the squiggles peppering the text of the advanced Vietnamese class and nearly resorting to a series of sad emoticons on the written placement examination, I was demoted, defeated, and asked to settle for the beginner class: the alphabet, the translations of food items, and the list of survival questions. The second thing I learned in Vietnamese class was my nationality. Người Mỹ, I repeated, class after class, the teacher calling on the prodigal Việt Kiều to demonstrate the down-tone of người, the nuanced wave of Mỹ, and the use of both words when describing our respective American selves. Five of six were impressed by how quickly I learned. I, still unable to articulate a Vietnamese story beyond being Jennifer, being an American, being a student, and being hungry, was concerned by how slowly I had progressed.

The third thing I learned in Vietnamese class was how to swap money for food. A few Vietnamese đồng or tiền, could purchase a pig's thịt lợn, a cow's thịt bò, a chicken's thịt gà, and a porcupine's thịt nhím. We listed the possibilities on the board, the scrap of the chalk recording every fruit, vegetable, and conceivably edible animal that came to our American minds. Five of six pens frantically scribbled the extensive vocabulary. I occasionally touched pen to paper for a monkey's thịt khỉ, among other items my mother could not stir fry, stew, or caramelize over a stove in Texas.

One of the last things I learned in Vietnamese class was the countries of the world. The teacher pointed to the east of Việt Nam, to Campuchia and to Thái Lan. She moved north to the vast, infamous lands of Trung Quốc. Her fingers crossed the ocean to the west, tracing over the shape that had become synonymous with Nước Mỹ, America. Six of six attentively watched the traversing of land and water, as we slowly eased into a conversation on du lịch, on travel. I practiced the pronunciation of the countries, training my tongue for words unfamiliar to my conversational vernacular, strangers to the empty pages of my new American passport.

Of all the terms, I glided effortlessly over two:

Nước Mỹ. Việt Nam.

"She should learn," my host mother would plead. "She's real Vietnamese."

"No she's not," my host sister would sigh. "She's Việt Kiều."

Normally a patient tutor to my Vietnamese questions, Vi would become flustered after an hour of describing and diagramming on the living room couch. The sheets of notebook paper would lay scattered on the floor as the French dialogue from the television began to blend with the backdrop of motorcycle hums and cricket chirps. Her extensive explanations, mixing Vietnamese, English and slipped trickles of French, would repeat a second, third, or fourth time. One night, after noticing my persistent trend of arriving home with a mortified glare, a sweat-slicked glow, and a disheveled head of hair, my host mother asked Vi to draw a map. On the note card were the post office, the school, and the hospital connected by a series of thickly-scored arrows. Vi handed the card to me, dictating right, left, right, phải, trái, phải until we both tired of directions, until we settled for writing the Vietnamese equivalent of "if found, please call..." on the back.

"She should learn. She's real Vietnamese."

Halfway through my stay in Vietnam, my host mother insisted that I learn the fourteen Vietnamese pronouns. The pronoun designation fluctuated to reflect the gender, relation, and age of the recipient, requiring either the astute observation of a seasoned Vietnamese or an elaborate chart carried by an amateur. Vi linked the fluid labels on paper and attempted to guide me through the boxes and lines with the tip of her pen. Mợ was the pronoun for a woman marrying my mother's younger brother. Mợ, I repeated, the word flowing as easily as it did during Christmas, Tết, and graduations. Chú was the pronoun for a man marrying my father's older sister. Chú, I rehearsed, the dip thong as unfamiliar as the side of the family I had never met. Em họ was the pronoun for the daughter of the woman marrying my mother's brother. Em họ, I tediously uttered, aware that I would be relegated to using Emily, Ashleigh, or Taylor. There was no pronoun for a man marrying my father's younger brother.

Noticing the decimation of both the chart and my attention span by the diagramming of the tenth pronoun, Vi left the chart incomplete, soliciting a real Vietnamese protest from my host mother. Vi slid the chart into my hands.

"No she's not. She's Việt Kiều."

The night before an examination, I practiced the geography of the world with Vi, weaving the vocabulary into phrases and commands. To Vi's nods, I adequately went to Thái Lan, visited Campuchia, and traveled to Trung Quốc. My host mother watched attentively, interrupting the sequence of my verbal globetrot upon arrival at Vietnam. We paused, anticipating slang, an idiom, or a colloquialism.

"She doesn't have to say go to Vietnam," she corrected her daughter, her eyes on the Việt Kiều.

"She can say go home to Việt Nam."

Remembering Things : 10 years with Vietnam

By: Philip Arthur Moore

September 25th, 2003

"While in Vietnamese class, my thầy told me that I've been reading well and that made me feel good. I know that I have a lot of work to do with the language and know that sometimes I forget how to give even a simple hello, how are you, but I'm trying my best."

September 29th, 2003

"Today I submitted my final piece of the study abroad application that I've been working on: a $45.00 check and a figurative farewell to the States. Let's hope I get in man."

November 18th, 2003

"I got a letter in the mail today notifying me that I have been awarded a scholarship for study abroad in Vietnam next semester; thank god for people willing to put faith in the desire of the youth to learn. I'm so lucky."

December 7th, 2003

"Yesterday I attended a study abroad orientation. Of the things I learned, the most I took out of the meeting was that I would be shell-shocked and homesick at times."

February 18th, 2004

Daddy never supported my decision to go. He had given me a large pocket knife the previous Christmas and I'd made the mistake of not only storing it in a carry-on but telling the Singapore Airlines agent at LAX that there were no sharp objects inside of my luggage.

This error in judgment at twenty-one years old in a post-9/11 America nearly prevented me from making my flight to Ho Chi Minh City. I was the last passenger to board SQ12, visibly shaken by a mean TSA interrogation and winded by a full sprint to my gate. My lasting memories from that moment were relief and sadness. I was on my plane with thirty hours of travel ahead of me and no tangible keepsake from my father.

It wasn't until just before he died that he finally began to accept that Vietnam wasn't a phase or random act of asserted independence. He never acknowledged the importance this country had in developing my manhood and I suspect it was in part because he thought I loved Vietnam more than him. I can't recall us ever having a conversation about my life here that didn't end with "When are you coming home?"

June 3rd, 2004

"Tonight I said goodbye to the Spring 2004 study abroad students with no more than a nod of acknowledgement and 'if it matters, I know we'll meet again...' 'cuz that's life. If it matters, it will happen."

Cần Thơ

I returned to the United States during the summer of 2004 and knew that I wouldn't stick around Rice University long. I wanted to quit. I hated everything about my first two years at the school: the drinking; my academic underachievement; how lonely and depressed I always felt; how I was never fully comfortable in my own skin to be my authentic self. My future was full of best guesses and failed attempts at sticking to one field of study. One year I wanted to be an engineer, the next a doctor, and the next a lawyer.

Were it not for Asian Studies I do not think that I would have ever graduated from Rice. It was the one field that I knew for a fact was a poor career decision—but the one field that gave me joy. Reading about and studying Vietnam kept me connected to the place when I wasn't here. I had all but emotionally checked out of my life at

Rice, and whatever I could do to finish up there while not losing hold of Vietnam I would do. So I bided my time in Houston during the second half of 2004 and returned here at the beginning of 2005, happy to be away from Texas again.

It was in 2005 that I became a part of my homestay sister's family. When I talk about family in Vietnam, she's who I am talking about. It's been nine years and I've been there for the entire duration of her children's lives. I love her, her husband, and her children like they are blood.

In Cần Thơ I feel so special and loved.

God's Death

Two events in my life have completely broken me. One was the death of my father on November 24th, 2009. He was found by my older brother with a laceration on his face. An autopsy performed three-and-a-half hours after his passing revealed the cause of death to be hypertensive cardiomyopathy alongside the presence of alcohol and alprazolam. The laceration likely happened against a coffee table after he stumbled and fell.

He was 55 years old and on November 28th, 2009, he was buried.

The three days between when he died and when we said goodbye to him were numb. I was so crippled with shock that I wasn't able to process what was happening. All I could focus on was buying a matching belt, pants, and coat set for his funeral. I couldn't give any attention to the fact that our last ever in-person meeting ended in another fight about Vietnam.

My relationship with my father was fractured and complicated. I moved out of his house at 14 and didn't speak to him again until I was 18. At 19, I moved from Longview, Texas, to Houston, Texas, for college, and at 21 I left for Vietnam. Between 5 and 14 I spent some time with him and some time with my mother. He simply wasn't around for the big changes, like the weight loss or the move to New York for a summer job or the move to another country. I tried my best to keep him up to date via my brother and sister, who have always lived in Texas, but our relationship was complicated. The last stable, happy memory I have of us together is from when I was a young child.

Still, he was my God and the closest thing to absolute authority that I will ever know. I feared him with every fiber of my being and respected him. He was more powerful than any other man I've ever met and the reason why I have a problem blindly taking orders from anyone.

My father was so flawed in so many ways—but so am I—and I suspect that the reason we rarely sat in harmony is that we both demanded respect from each other. Respect is more valuable to me than money, status, or material goods. It has either made or ruined every relationship that has mattered.

Before dying my father told me that the reason we had a troubled life together was because we were one and the same. We fought in our own ways, his through sheer fury and mine through deafening silence. He yelled whenever he was angry. I walk away and shut people out. Both killed us.

After his death my best friend saw me through two-and-a-half years of crippling anxiety, panic, and depression, trying to pick up the pieces around me. You learn who your friends are when panic and anxiety take over your life. They remind you time and time again that things will be okay.

I lost a few close friends in the States after his death because I felt like they didn't care about how much I was suffering. It was one of the weakest moments of my life and a few friends who I thought cared couldn't be bothered to check in on me.

The ones who were in Vietnam called and the ones who I'd met in Vietnam and had returned to their countries called. The ones living closest to me didn't. That hurt.

Hanoi

The first time that I ever came to Hanoi was in 2004 with my study abroad group. I hated it here. I didn't like the people, the culture, the food, the weather, or anything about the lakes. I had grown so in love with my time in Saigon and had been so influenced by my Vietnamese friends in the States and Vietnam that the thought of living in Hanoi had never crossed my mind. Still, after my father's death and having been away from Vietnam for a year I knew that I needed to return.

When I returned to Hanoi six years after first visiting things had changed. I no longer enjoyed Saigon and thought that the city was too crowded and too hectic for a peaceful life. My father's death had made me colder and harder, which seemed to work more suitably with Hanoians. The lakes here gave me a sense of stability; they were so still and calm. The weather became a constant topic of conversation, which I enjoyed. The women cared and talked about things that I cared and talked about. The food wasn't sugary like it was in the south. There was so much culture, both foreign and local. Things felt good.

It's hard to reflect on a time that's just passed. It's so difficult to put in perspective the last few years and I think that ten years from now I may be able to look back on recent memory with a more objective and surgical approach. What I do know, though, is that something has changed.

I'm not sure when or how but something has changed. I used to ask myself daily if Vietnam would continue to be a part of my life. I thought that staying in Vietnam was failing and that leaving my country was wrong. I tried a move to San Francisco because that's what successful technology people are supposed to do. I wasn't able to shake the many years that my father questioned my wanting to be in Vietnam. I no longer feel this way.

The last few years were a blur, mostly due to work and travel. It will take some time to figure them out but I took from them that the United States is my birth place, but I no longer see it as a place in which I will want to settle down again. It's hard to tell other Americans that our country isn't for me.

July 9th, 2014.

I turned thirty-three in Vietnam today and I feel old. I've been feeling this way for a while now. I'm called older brother and uncle a lot more. Strangers ask me why I haven't married anyone yet. Friends are having babies.

Ten years ago it would not have been unusual for someone to ask me if one of my goals in Vietnam was to find a girlfriend and bring her back to the United States. I joke now that my goal is to marry my way into being able to live here forever.

Things feel slower. Traffic doesn't move as quickly as it used to. Miscommunications don't happen as frequently as they did a while back.

July 20th, 2014.

When I was twenty-one years old I came to Vietnam. I'm much older now and haven't quite left. There've been a few extended returns to the United States during that time but for the most part my life has centered around this country.

With the exception of my immediate biological family and a few close friends, America doesn't play a very large role in my life anymore. I don't know if it ever will again. It took me many years to have peace with my decision to move away from my country and I've only recently found the confidence to discuss this with my family without hedging my bets or avoiding hurting their feelings. I do not move back. I visit as much as I can.

Time has given me memories in Vietnam. I dream and love in both English and Vietnamese. I've learned things here and become a man here. Sometimes I open old journals to understand how far I've come.

[Philip is African-American by birth, but he is as Vietnamese as the rest of us. Having spent the last 10 years in Vietnam, he speaks fluently. Vietnam is his home. He is truly a brother from another mother.

This is an partial excerpt from an excellent piece found on his medium at: https://medium.com/@philip_arthur.]

Brothers

By: Huy T. Pham

I used to mock the students who just came from Vietnam. I would laugh at their elementary grasp of English. But, when they saw me, they would smile, they would wave their hands in the air, and they would shout "Anh Huy! Anh Huy!". I remember thinking to myself, "Don't call me your brother. I am not your brother." And as others looked on, I would look them straight in the eye and say, "Go back to Vietnam. Go back to where you belong."

I was impossible. Rather than study Vietnamese at the Catholic church, as soon as the nun turned to write on the board, I would jump out of the window and run to the arcade. Forget my heritage. Street Fighter was more important.

I am a Vietnamese American, but like most of my generation, I am forever attempting to grasp the meaning of my heritage. But I am trying. In March 2006, I joined a work camp in Vietnam, building elementary school classrooms.

As much as I believe in the cause, it was the Vietnamese volunteers I spent every waking hour with that left the most profound effect. The volunteers were my age and they were the most charming, hospitable people I have ever met. Despite the fact that I was a "Viet Kieu" (Vietnamese overseas), they treated me as an old friend, taking me out on the town almost every night. We spent hours in deep conversation talking about opportunities they may never experience.

I could have been one of them. I won't ever forget that. A difference of a few minutes during my parents' escape, and I would have been lucky to be as educated and accomplished as my friends in Vietnam. Chances are I would've dropped out of school to help with the family fishing business.

In the past few years, I've uncovered the true treasure of the Vietnamese people. I've had hot soy milk overlooking the majestic mountains of Dalat. I've had iced coffee on the pure beaches of Nha Trang. I've bathed in the mud baths and hot springs of Thap Ba. I've shopped at the floating market of Vung Tau. But I've realized that the true treasure of the Vietnamese people isn't found in the material world – it lies within us. We possess an indomitable spirit like no other.

Whether it manifests in Vietnamese American parents working long hours at jobs they are overly qualified for, students in Vietnam going to classes in despicable conditions, or soldiers fighting an impossible war – our indomitable spirit extends across generations, oceans and language barriers. We are brothers and sisters. Family is there for one another. Always.

I'm a different man than I was years ago. I am thankful for the first hand experiences I've had, for there is no better teacher. I've been taught the richness and beauty of a culture that I once was too young to appreciate. I will continue to learn. I will continue to volunteer my time in helping Vietnamese people all over the world. But more importantly – I will try to be a better brother.

Editor's Note

I hope you enjoyed the _I Am Vietnamese_ anthology. I wanted to make this anthology edgy, real, and raw. Together we did it! This was a pipe dream that became a reality with the support of people like you.

Looking back, my only regret is that I chose the wrong title. It should not be _I Am Vietnamese_, but rather _We Are Vietnamese_. Not just one person, but a family. We are a community like no other. A people without a land. Yet, our spirit remains indomitable. In our hearts, if nowhere else, we are Vietnamese.

As you struggle with your Vietnamese identity, never think that you are alone. You are always supported by your fellow Vietnamese brothers and sisters. We understand what you are going through. I hope this anthology proves that.

If you enjoyed this anthology, feel free to reach out to me at huy@iamvietnamese.org.

Charities

The Vietnamese Culture and Science Association (VCSA)

http://www.vcsa.org

The Vietnamese Culture and Science Association (VCSA) is a non-profit 501(c)(3) Vietnamese American organization founded in 1990. It has over 500 members, mostly young Vietnamese American professionals in the US and Canada. Based in Houston, Texas, VCSA has chapters in Austin, Dallas/Fort Worth, San Diego, Washington DC, Minneapolis/St. Paul and Toronto.

"We promote excellence in education, leadership and skills development through culture and science. Our organization encourages multi-generational and cross-cultural collaborations. We foster civic participation in the mainstream and Vietnamese America."

SUNFLOWER MISSION

http://www.sunflowermission.org

Sunflower Mission is a 501(c)(3) organization committed to improving the lives of the people in Vietnam, mainly through educational assistance programs. We are an U.S.-based, non-profit, non-political, non-governmental organization.

"We seek to improve the future of Vietnam, one student at a time. We are bringing school facilities, teaching and learning materials, and assistance to education to Vietnam.

We are doing the work to assist and oversee the completion of projects in selected areas, where school facilities or resources are minimal or non-existent.

Sunflower Mission's hands-on involvement with these projects ensures that the funds are directed to the intended targets.

We improve the lives of the students and communities that we served. Our students finish primary and secondary education and continue to pursue higher education. We form strong and trusting bonds with all we helped. Our students become successful volunteers, teachers, and leaders."

The Vietnamese American Scholarship Foundation (VASF)

http://www.vietscholarships.org

The Vietnamese American Scholarship Foundation (VASF) believes that every student deserves an opportunity to achieve academic, personal, and professional success regardless of financial, ethnic, or family background. VASF provides Vietnamese American students with additional resources and support to help students become high-achieving and civic-minded leaders.

"We recognize that access to higher education is fundamental to a balanced perspective and to success as a community leader. VASF serves as a resource for the Vietnamese American community by providing a framework for others to invest in potential future leaders through the creation of scholarships, fellowships, and mentoring and leadership programs. The Vietnamese American Scholarship Foundation has been helping Vietnamese American students pursue their dreams since 2003."

[This page left intentionally blank.]

CPSIA information can be obtained
at www.ICGtesting.com
Printed in the USA
FSOW01n2303270115
4828FS